MY DEEPEST HEART'S DEVOTIONS

AN AFRICAN WOMAN'S DIARY - BOOK 1

GERTRUDE KABATALEMWA

Edited by NONA BABICH AND TERESA SKINNER
Photography by ALISA ALBERS
Photography by TERESA SKINNER

ISBN: 978-1-950123-17-9

Copyright © 2019 by Teresa Skinner

Unless otherwise indicated, all Scripture quotations are taken from the Holy Bible, King James Version - Public Domain Scripture quotations marked (ESV) ® Bible (The Holy Bible, English Standard Version®), copyright © 2001 by Crossway, a publishing ministry of Good News Publishers. Used by permission. All rights reserved."

Scripture quotations marked (NIV) are taken from the Holy Bible, New International Version®, NIV®. Copyright © 1973, 1978, 1984, 2011 by Biblica, Inc.™ Used by permission of Zondervan. All rights reserved worldwide. www.zondervan.com The "NIV" and "New International Version" are trademarks registered in the United States Patent and Trademark Office by Biblica, Inc.™

All rights reserved.

No part of this book may be reproduced in any form or by any electronic or mechanical means, including information storage and retrieval systems, without written permission from the publisher, except for the use of brief quotations in a book review.

Gone so soon,
with all the dedicated work she had done...
we will continue with the work she has left behind.
showing people "God's Love and Care"
Emmanuel Mwesigye

CONTENTS

Foreword   xi

1. Saints must walk alone   1
2. A Pilgrim's Prayer   5
3. Nyamabuga would be A Spring Board   9
4. Lord Help Me to Mark What I See   11
5. Our Lord's Way to Save Us Was Not Easy   17
6. Sic Transit Gloria Mundi   25
7. God Destined Uganda as a Missionary Nation   31
8. Way-Laying God, Trapping God (Kutega Mukama)   33
9. I Have Been Waiting for You to Take This Step   41
10. The Call   43
11. You are an Original   51
12. Bondages and Prison   59
13. Deep Well of My Heart   71
14. Conference of Youthful Married Couples   73
15. Why is Satan Fighting the Church, and Not Jesus?   83
16. End Time Spiritual Warfare   87
17. Call Upon the Lord   95
18. A Wise Man   97
19. My Purpose Driven Life   101
20. Characteristics of Worship that Please God   117
21. The Best Way to Spell Love is "T I M E,"   121
22. Where Do I Draw My Strength?   125
23. Inner Peace   127
24. Kyabarokole Church Conference   135
25. Set Yourself Free   149
26. Blasphemous and Abusive Songs   151
27. End Time, Spiritual WarFare,   157
28. I Can Steal That Sheep From You   163
29. My Friend - Who is the Wicked Person?   165

30. The Truly Spiritual Man   171

    About the Author   179

WORD OF THE LORD FOR GERTRUDE KABATALEMWA

I believe I heard the Lord say
You are a General - in His army
You are a woman of valor
You are a woman of great faith
Those who have preceded you and those that will follow

There is not one with a greater faith as you
You are an Apostle - there will be more churches established
Training up those in your care now to begin other church groups
As His message of salvation and love continues to be spread
throughout the nation

I believe I heard the Lord say
Your job is not done
You have accomplished much but
There is much more to be accomplished
He has given you a great vision
And those to stand with you in bringing forth this vision
You cannot do this alone

I believe I heard Him say
Begin to seek Him
There are those who are now working in various projects
But He will begin to show you - one by one-
Those whom He will raise up to walk beside you
To further along and to fulfill the vision
Walking with you in unity, harmony and one accord
To accomplish the same vision He has given you
You to delegate responsibility for various projects to those He shows you
So that you can be freed up to begin new endeavors
And to further along others

Multiplication - multiplication of help - more people to be set in place to help you
To take on more of the work that needs to be done
Delegation - your delegating more work to others to free up yourself

He will continue to provide for you
Finances help in all you need
The vision is expanding
More will be started
More will be accomplished

And I believe I hear the Lord say
The angels of the Lord encamp around you
And continue to be at your side
To protect you and provide for the needs
Rest in peace knowing that even greater things are in store
Greater things will be accomplished

And I believe I hear the Lord say

You have been found faithful
He loves you very much

And the Lord says to you
"Well done My good and faithful servant!"

Sunday Mar 28, 2010 Approximately 5:20 PM

FOREWORD

We may not agree with what Ms. Gertrude Kabatalemwa has written. It may not be politically correct for our generation. But, let us get passed our judgements, and hear the heart of this African woman.

If so, we will find ourselves understanding a depth of spirituality that will most likely be lost to the next generations.

AFRICA HAS SOMETHING TO SAY TO US.

May we listen intently with raw ears to hear a direction that could keep our future from becoming sterile.

Teresa Skinner
All Nations International

CHAPTER 1
SAINTS MUST WALK ALONE

IN THE DOMAIN of the Kingdom of Darkness there is fear, oppression and bondage in the Kingdom of God there is Faith and Freedom

- Every day we are either taking ground or losing it in fight for the eternity.
- God gave man Freedom to Worship Him harmoniously from his Free Will, or else He could have created computers and program them to worship Him.
- Where the Spirit of the Lord is, there is "LIBERTY" Corinth. 3:17 NOT "Where the Spirit is Lord, there is LIBERTY.
- The tree of Knowledge of Good and Evil was placed in the Garden for Adam and Eve to prove obedience and Love for God. Therefore, every temptation and trial in our lives has the same purpose.
- The Lord wants us to worship Him

- Spirit where the Still Small Voice of the Lord is over shadowed.

NOISE MESSAGE GOD GAVE ME

SAINTS MUST WALK ALONE.

Whoever has passed on into the divine Presence the actual Inner experience will not find many who understand her/him. She will mix with religious persons in fellowship, but true spiritual fellowship will be hard to find. After all he is as stranger and a Pilgrim. The journey she takes is not on her/his feet but in her heart. She walks with God in the Garden of her own soul, but who can walk with her there but God. She is of another Spirit from the multitude that tread the courts of the Lord's house, not from the noisy world of gossip and, rumour mongering.

THE TRULY SPIRITUAL MAN IS ODD/STRANGE, NOT UNDERSTOOD, MISTAKEN ALWAYS:

- Lives not for self.
- Promotes the interest of others.
- Pleads to people to give all to the Lord.
- Asks no portion or share for self
- Delights not to be honoured but
- To see the Saviour glorified in the eyes of others

- The Lord promoted and self-neglected
- Is often silent in the midst of NOISE religious shop talk. For this is earnest
- Referred as dull and over serious, a gulf between her and society widens.
- Searchers for friends of the same mind and finds few or none, like Mary
- of the old keeps these things in her heart.
- Seeks to understand the Saviour more intimately
- Heartbroken for the Lord and after righteousness
- Has many trials but not shaken by them, eyes fixed on the Lord
- Is a topic of everybody, as they seek to break into their secret cover
- Is not easily penetrated, safeguards the Lord's Secrets
- Has on, a robe of humility which attracts no one but only the Giver
- Self-denial for the sake of seeking righteousness
- Does not discuss affairs of others for slander.
- Cares for the interest of others
- Is fulfilled when others are happy

Just before young Peter was kidnapped

CHAPTER 2

A PILGRIM'S PRAYER

O! Lord, I have heard your voice and was afraid and humbled. It is you who have called me to a great task in a grave, terrible and rebellious hour. You are about to shake Nations, earth and also heaven; except heaven cannot be shaken.

O! Lord, my Lord, you have stood to honour me to be your Maid Servant. No man takes this honour upon himself, only he that is called of God, as was Aaron.

> *You have made me your Messenger to them that*
> *Are stubborn of heart and hard of hearing.*
>   *they have*
> *Rejected you their God and how will they receive*
>   *me a servant.*

My God, I shall not waste time complaining of my weakness or my inability for the work. The responsibility is not mine, but Yours, O! Lord. It is you who said "I know thee, I ordained thee, and I sanctified thee."

You also said "I shall go where ever you shall send me and

whatever You command me, I shall speak." Who am I to argue with You or to question your divine choice?

The decision is not mine but Yours. So be it, Lord, your Will not mine, be done. You, the God of the Prophets and the apostles, as long as I honour You, You will...

...Uplift me.

Help me therefore, to take this personal vow to honour You in all my future life, and labours, whether by gain or by loss by life or by death. To keep this vow unbroken, as long as I live.

TO KEEP THIS VOW UNBROKEN, AS LONG AS I LIVE.

It is time, O God, for You to work for the enemy has entered into Your pastures and the sheep are torn and scattered. And false shepherds who deny the danger laugh at the perils surrounding the flock.

The flock, Your people, are deceived by greedy shepherds, putting them to sleep with success messages and get rich quick schemes while the wolf closes in to kill and destroy. I beg You Lord, give me sharp eyes to detect the presence of the enemy, give me the understanding to see and courage to report what I see faithfully. Make my voice Your loud speaker so that even the sick people will recognize it and look to You.

Lord Jesus, I come to You for spiritual preparation. Lay Your hand upon me. Anoint me with the oil of the New Testament servant.

Forbid that I should become a religious fanatic and thus lose my calling. Save me from the curse that comes to modern Christians, the curse of compromising into sin of imitating others and of professionalism.

Save me from the error of judging people, the way they act, behave, judging a church by its size, its popularity or policy of offering. Help me to know that I am Your maid servant, not a promoter, not a religious manager, but a maid-servant.

LET ME NEVER BECOME A SLAVE TO CROWDS.

Let me never become a slave to crowds. Heal my soul of carnal ambitions and deliver me from the itch of publicity. Save me from bondage to material things. Lay Your terror upon me O God, and drive me to the corner of prayer where I may wrestle with principalities, powers and the rulers of darkness in this world.

Deliver me from over eating and waking up late. Teach me self-discipline that I may be a Good soldier of Jesus Christ. Help me to accept hard work and small rewards in this world. I ask no easy life. Block the highways and paths that could make life easier. If others seek a smoother path; let me take the hard way without judging them.

When opposition or argument about God comes my way, let me take it quietly with wisdom. If grateful gifts are given to me by Your faithful people, stand by me and save me from pride that often follows. Teach me to use whatever I receive in such manner that will not injure, hurt my soul, over shadow nor diminish my spiritual power.

And if in Your permissive providence honour should come to me from You, let me not count myself worthy of it, but of the least of Your mercies.

If men know me as intimately as I know myself, let their honours be bestowed upon others who are most worthy to receive them, not me.

Now, O Lord of heaven and earth I consecrate my remaining days to You. Let them be many or few as You will. Let me stand before the great or serve the poor and lowly, the choice is Yours and I would not influence it if I could.

I AM YOUR MAID SERVANT TO DO YOUR WILL

I am Your Maid Servant to do Your will, that will be sweeter to me than position, riches or fame and I choose it above all things on earth or in heaven. Though I am chosen of You and honoured by a high and holy calling, let me never forget that I am but a man of dust and ashes, a man of all the natural faults and passions that plagues the human race.

Therefore, Lord and Redeemer, save me from myself and from all the hurts and injuries I have and may cause myself while trying to be a blessing to others. Fill me with Your power by the Holy Spirit and I will go in Your power and strength to tell of Your righteousness.

I will spread abroad the message of redeeming love while my normal human powers endure. Then dear Lord, when I get old and weak to go on, have a place ready for me above, and make me to be numbered with Your saints in Glory everlasting. Amen. 25th December 1996

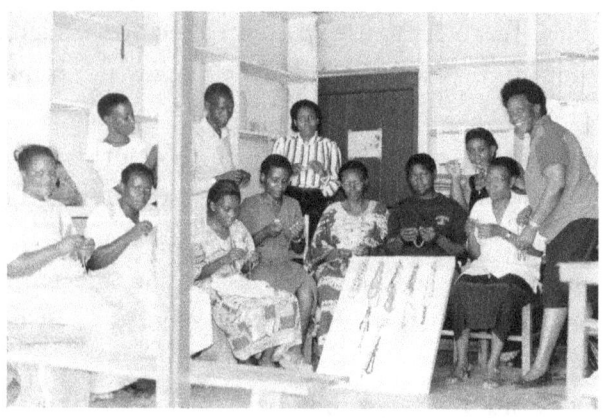

Gertrude teaching women to make necklaces

CHAPTER 3

NYAMABUGA WOULD BE A SPRING BOARD

WE HAD our 1st ever Seminar with the theme "But when the Perfect comes, the partial will be done away," 1 Corinthians 13:10. (Ekibi kitekwa Ekibi). Since the Children of God stood here and prophesied Nyamabuga has never been the same. Even what you are seeing here is the result of the Prophecies, which the Lord had earlier shown me, that Nyamabuga would be A Spring Board for Tooro Kingdom's deliverance.

MBALE NYAIBARA, SEMINAR - ROAD MARCH.

For our salvation, the Lord was Chastised, Isaiah 52:14,

> So, His appearance was marred more than the sons of men.

Those who try to stand in your way, leave them, forgive them and pray for them.

Give all your battles to God to Fight for you. If people knew the glory which was shown through the death of Jesus Christ it would be the highest wisdom for anyone to think about. To think of His suffering, there is power which can enable you to Fight all spiritual battles. Every day if you consider the truth in the death of Jesus Christ you will never be ashamed. Many want to know about the Grace, Forgiveness, Healing, and His Provisions but few want to think of His suffering. Satan gives fake Holy Fear, one says "I cannot see the Lord suffering," yet that is where you draw your strength.

If you take Grace, Forgiveness, Healing and Provisions for granted, you will be in danger of being deceived and fall out of Grace. We need to surrender our lives daily to our Lord. Many have fallen in the hands of wrong doctrines and cults, made to trust in water or drink concoctions, oil, etc. Many "Born Again Christians" have not trusted the Lord. They have gone to Japan, London, and America telling lies that they were persecuted in order to be accepted. They do odd jobs in mortuaries or clean toilets, yet their parents paid a lot of money for their education. 27th - 28th August 2007

I READ THE CALL BY RICK JOYNER.

Prayer, Lord, help me to understand what I see in my vision and destination. Help me to look for the path and means to reach my vision with righteousness. And to help me to make a Map of our daily walk including thoughts, words and places. Help me to avoid doors which are attractively, opened by the enemy, and lead me to see doors which are opened by You. Amen. 19th December 2007

CHAPTER 4

LORD HELP ME TO MARK WHAT I SEE

LORD HELP me to mark what I see in my vision (destination)

Help me to look for the path and means to reach there (Righteousness)

And to help me to make a map of daily walk (thoughts, words and walk)

Help me to avoid doors which are attractively, opened by the enemy...

And lead me to see doors which are opened by you. *19th December, 2007*

DEAR LORD I AM READY

Dear Lord I am ready, standing in your presence for your TAKE, you who Chose me before I was formed in the womb of my mother, you knew me Before I came into this world; here I am for YOU.

Lord you are a good keeper let me be for your KEEP, the one

you Choose to keep never regrets. You don't keep your people in delusion You keep them in the TRUTH, because you are TRUTH itself. You keep Your people for future betterment. You keep your people on ETERNAL PROMISES.

Lord you used many people to carry on your name, Abraham, Joseph, Moses, Elijah, Isaiah, Jeremiah of the old and in our days Smith Wigglesworth, Mary Etter, T.A Tozer and Joyce Meyer of today. May you please also USE me selfless for your own Glory. Sheave me, strain me, winnow me and leave me pure. *20th December 2007*

The false Wisdom, e.g. Doctrines or cults will lead you to bondage. Establish a pattern in your life, always choosing the highest and best way of doing things. There can be no victory without a battle and the greater the battle the greater the victory. The more victories you experience, the more you rise to face higher and bigger ones. *23rd December 2007*

DO NOT TO WASTE A SINGLE TRIAL

One of the first things we must learn on this journey is not to waste a single Trial, but to seize trials as opportunities to climb higher ladders. If your path is more difficult, it is because of your high calling. Yes!!! Discipline is the path that leads you to reach the mountain top. You should not be consumed with self or seek recognition, ambition or have pride in your walk. *24rd December 2007*

YOU MUST LEARN WHEN TO CAMP, WHEN TO MARCH, AND

how to Fight. You should do all these right and do them all well. You will Be ready to do each of these in season and out of season, and always do the right thing at the right time even if it may not seem right to you. 26rd *December 2007*

ALL OF THE TREASURES ON EARTH CANNOT OUTWEIGH IN A balance with the value of a single Soul of any man. Also if you put together all the riches of the whole world, they cannot be worth your soul for one second. He has made everything beautiful in its time. Also, he has put eternity into man's heart, yet so that he cannot find out what Go, has done from the beginning to the end, Eccl. 3:11. The Lord said I am building my City in the hearts of men, with the hearts of men.

NO WEAPON THAT IS FORMED AGAINST ME OR THEE WILL PROSPER, ISAIAH 54:7; AND NO WEAPON THE LORD GIVES ME WILL FAIL.

Each of my houses will fit perfectly into the land where they are located, not according to human measurements, but according to the Lord's way. The first skill that the Lord's builder should develop is the skill of surveying. They must know the land because the Lord says He designed the land for His people. When you build with Wisdom what you build will fit perfectly with the land, e.g. Amber House and GG Tower.

GOD'S GENERALS

> I can see the future far more clearly than I can solve the mysteries of the immediate present.
>
> ALEXANDER DOWIE

Even though we are called we still have to war against spiritual evil that are sent to destroy our vision and to discourage us.

We must learn that it is not always right to move into action, because it seems like the thing you want to do. The kind of obedience only comes from seasons of prayer and intercession in the closet with your creator.

Only people whose hearts are changed by the gospel can transform civil laws and regulations. The apostolic and politics don't mix.

> Learn How to live out of the Spirit while resting your body at the same time.
>
> CORRIE TEN BOOM

This is when you feel you want to pray but you are tired, you go to sleep and cover yourself with the blood of Jesus until when you are revived both Spiritually and Physically then you pray with understanding.

The things of God are not like the things of secular world!!!!!!!!!!

In becoming an apostle, it is not a question of rising high, it is a question to becoming low enough.

...IT IS NOT A QUESTION OF RISING HIGH, IT IS A QUESTION TO BECOMING LOW ENOUGH.

Prayer, Lord, let me reach enough depth of true humility, of true bottom and self-effacement, for attaining the high office of being an apostle. Amen.

Jesus never commanded us to build communes, He commanded us to "Go!", not "Huddle," Acts 2:44-47; 5:1-10; 8:1 - so, the Great Commission Matt. 28:19-20.

One of the great snares comes in today's teaching in the form of Power and Success. Success brings a multitude of unholy venues and ventures. We can fall victim to protocol or into traps of whirl-wind ventures through vast selections teaching of success and power. Never be afraid of success, but to properly administer success, we must hold ourselves in the strength of the Spirit and listen to His direction, not our own. Through the Holy Spirit's strength and a hunger for God we are able to continue to the next level. When we obey God success just comes, 2 Chronicles 9:22 and 17:5.

We must remain with the original, anointed plan of God for our lives and allow Him to show us how to administrate it regarding Schools, Vocational Bible Training and Vocational Training Colleges. *27rd December 2007*

Son, Peter, second man from the right, returned 20 years later after being kidnapped

CHAPTER 5

OUR LORD'S WAY TO SAVE US WAS NOT EASY

AFTER A LONG NIGHT with the Lord in my quiet time I read in A.W. Tozer "Nearness and Likeness." He said, "People or Christians think that God is far from them but in actual sense they are the ones who are far from God."

THE TRUTH MUST ENTER THE MIND BEFORE IT CAN ENTER the heart, e.g. in Spiritual matters we think correctly only when we boldly rule out the concept of Space. God is a Spirit and a Spirit dwells not in space, space is to do with matter, and Spirit is independent of it. Space accounts for the relation of material bodies to each other. Never think God is partially near or far, He is not here or there, but He carries here and there in His heart.

Space is not infinite, only God is infinite, in His infinitude He swallows up all space because He is the one who created it. "Do I not fill heaven and earth?" saith the Lord. As the ocean fills the bucket that is submerged in it, as the ocean submerges the bucket, so does God in the universe He fills, "Why? Even the heaven and the heaven of heavens cannot contain You," the Heaven of

Heavens cannot contain thee. God is not contained; He contains, 2 Chronicles 6.

God created us Living Souls in a body in order to experience the world and communicate with one another; Man is a Soul, having a body, or living in a body, not a Body having a Soul.

God is near to all parts of His Universe, Psalm 139:1-18. Some people experience His nearness and others do not because of dissimilarity and not being Godlike which creates closeness or distance.

Two creatures may be so close physically that they touch, e.g. different animals in the national park, people in marriage that you find each one is millions of miles apart; or angel and an ape may be in the same room-but living apart from each other.

We are living, moving and our being is in God. God is nearer to us than we are to ourselves. "I love this Lord."

Thinking stirs feelings and feelings trigger Action.

Thinking about God and Holy things creates a moral climate favourable to the growth of faith, love, humility and reverence. Spirit inspired thinking helps to make our minds pure sanctuaries in which God will be pleased to dwell.

Consider what you thought about when you were free to think; did that please you? When the bird of thought was let go did it fly out like the raven to settle upon floating carcasses or circle and return like the dove to the ark of God?

We should train our thoughts by long periods of daily prayer. Long practice in the art of mental prayer, that is talking to God inwardly as we work or travel. This will form the habit of Holy Thoughts. *6th January 2008*

PEOPLE HAVE DECIDED TO LOOK FOR EASY LIFE AND FORGOT THAT OUR LORD'S WAY TO SAVE US WAS NOT EASY

People have decided to look for easy life and forgot that our Lord's way to save us was not easy; He sweated blood, His body was marred, He was spit upon, He went naked and later was crucified for our sake, Isaiah 52:13-15. One pastor's wife was preaching and said "When we are saved, we should not be hated." That means no suffering, no persecution, remembering our brothers and sisters in China. God dealt with him to the point where he was forced to redefined some of his criteria for what it means to be "Saved."

"If it takes the perfection of environment to prove the presence of God in your life," the persecuted Christians just do not have God. How can they?

They do not have Bible seminars, they do not have Mass Choirs or the latest worship music. They do not have air conditioning, ushers, nurseries, electronic paging systems, carpeted sanctuaries or counselors. Their worship environment is terrible. One group of Chinese Christians who were caught holding a Church Service and Officials placed a horse pipe through in the middle of town and forced every man and woman in that congregation to urinate into it. Then they drowned the Pastor in it, right in front of their eyes.

BRO TOMMY TENNY, THE GOD CHASERS

But remember Jesus said You will be hated for my sake. If I was hated you will also be hated.

"Earth's crammed with heaven, And every common bush afire with God, But only he who sees takes off his shoes;The rest sit round and pluck blackberries."— Elizabeth Barrett Browning

---

A single Word of God is worth more than all of the treasure on earth! Because it is power, it is living and it's created the World.

...TELL ME ABOUT THE SIGNPOSTS THAT WILL SHOW ME I AM STILL ON THE RIGHT PATH.

May the Holy Spirit lead me. Amen.

When we go to the hospital, school, Church, etc. you will find a sign post which will lead you to the right place. Without a sign post you will get lost; on some sign posts you find a pointing arrow showing you the direction.

We need a sign post to let us know that we are on the right path. There is many times the Lord is come to us to warn us in thoughts, i.e. on 4th July 2008 there was a plan to steal my truck. At 7.00pm I left a meeting at Uganda Orphans Relief Fund in Zane. On the way I branched off to put in fuel at former Caltex Petrol Station, now Total Station. Opposite Uganda House the Lord asked me "Where are you going?" He revealed to me the plan of the kidnappers.

God sends His Word or He sends you a person to tell you what is going wrong; i.e. a story of Brother Bill. Early in 1984 God sent me to warn Bill, a Born-Again Christian, that his walk was in danger. We used to attend the same Church. The Lord sent me to warn him. In a dream I saw Bill with a well-known outgoing town woman. She was later infected with AIDS after being with so many rich and high government officials who returned from a guerrilla war. But the Lord knew it and wanted to save Bill. In a dream I saw him stealthily giving a bottle of beer to that lady and trying to hid it from me. When he saw me coming he pretended he had done nothing but I had noticed what he had done. I heard the voice of God saying "Tell Bill to leave Rose, (not the real name) GO and tell him."

I woke up shaking, and I told the Lord "I am not married, and Bill is a divorcee, he will think I am trying to make a pass at him." The Lord said, "Go tell him." I asked for the sign which tells me that he will not think wrong about me. The Lord put me in a trance, I saw myself in the Wandegeya Market yard, Bill came up driving a lemon green Mercedes Benz, got out and stood at a distance, I went running to tell him of the dream, a dream in a Dream. I woke up. The Lord said, "Go and Tell him." I said, Lord, I ask you; tomorrow when I go to the office if I call him and tell him I have a message for you! He will come immediately without a question. Bill was a respectable man, of the same as a minister. He could not obey my command and come where I was, but I could go to him if I had anything to tell him.

Early in the morning, it was a Monday morning, at 8.00am I looked up his telephone number in the phone book, found his name and called him. I was precise and concise; I saluted him: "Praise the Lord Bro Bill, I have a message for you from the Lord." I am here at Parliament 3rd Floor in Room 19. He said, "I will be there in a minute."

When he came, I told him exactly how I saw it, and what the Lord told me to tell him. "Leave Rose." He cried real tears and told me that he was a real friend to her, in order to make her a Christian so he could marry her. He left my office. I did not know anything about Bill and Rose, but in that dream that night the Lord gave me her name and I saw her in a dream.

Around December the same year, we were having a Morris Cerullo Conference at Mwiri, in Jinja, after picking Dr. Alexander Ness who was presenting Bro Morris Cerullo, from the Airport, we got so busy, as I was one of the organizers, I slept very late.

Immediately when I put my head on the pillow, the Lord came, He said "Go and tell Bill if he is not going to leave Rose, I will pluck Rose's eyes out, and also his, and they will both walk blind." I was so scared. We spent a week at Mwiri for the Conference, when it was over the day was Thursday; on Friday morning I went straight to see Bill. When I appeared on the door way he said, "I know why you are here." He gave me a seat and I told him exactly what the Lord said. He had no words, he had continued with her despite the warning God gave him. Later the lady had a plane crash in Italy in 1990 and did not die; but died later of AIDS. Before she died she wrote a list of the people she passed the disease to and also Bro Bill died of AIDS in 2009.

NOT ONLY DOES HE GIVE US SIGNPOSTS ABOUT WARNING, BUT ALSO WHEN YOU PLEASE HIM

He tells you about the signpost that leads you to a reward awaiting; i.e. in a dream in 1983 there was a burning fire; Jane, Josephine and I was in the storm. There was a fire place where we had to run a marathon to find our fire before it went out. In this dream of the old man there was a hand of God stirring fire and everyone had to gird himself and go through that fire.

Well, we all need a sign post to let us know that we are on the right path. Many people have ignored the sign posts and got lost. For one to get lost, it does not come abruptly, but he goes out gradually, until he finds he has gone very far, beyond return.

King Asa of Judah loved God for 35 years and was at peace and had no war. He relaxed, when he came to the 36th year Israel attacked him. he never turned to the Lord but he consulted the doctors, 2 Chronicles 16:19. Instead of trusting God he trusted king Hadad for protection. When prophet Hananiah came to warn him, he threw him in prison and became rigid. Even when he got sick, he never turned to the Lord but he consulted the doctors.

Learn to listen to that still small voice. People have lost or are going to lose eternity just because of lacking obedience, having laziness or pride. When the call comes and the door opens they do not enter immediately. The reason being that they are busy or not ready; when they make up their mind to answer the call, it's too late, the door is closed. Same with blessings, many times blessings come in a way you do not realize, they are an opened door, i.e. story of a man who had prayed for a long time for an open door, but when it opened, he lost the blessings because of pride and arrogance.

This man prayed and prayed for a financial open door, but one day the Lord heard his prayers. As he was sitting on his verandah, he saw a person who came to him and handed him an envelope with big money. He could not believe his eyes and he asked him if the money was truly sent to him and who sent it? But the messenger told him not to worry, take the money, it is yours. The one who sent me told me to give it to you and it is yours. This person came at a certain time of day for three consecutive days bringing the same amount of money. The praying man, getting used to receiving the money, told the messenger that tomorrow when you come, I will not be around, I have a journey to make. When you come slip the envelope under the door. The messenger asked, "Can't you postpone that journey?" He said no, I have to go. So, he went and when the messenger came the next day he passed by his home and gave the envelope to the next home owner. When the foolish man came back and looked under the door, there was no envelope. So, he decided to wait until the next day. As he was waiting at exact time the messenger came as usual but he saw him passing by going to the next home. He ran to him and said "You are lost, you are supposed to come to me." The messenger answered him "Sorry you lost your chance, you could not wait, but there was another person who was in need." (Kola Ngabulijjo story) *19th April 2008*

CHAPTER 6

SIC TRANSIT GLORIA MUNDI

THE PEOPLE who know God's will show great exploitations, display strength and take action, i.e. Daniel 11:32.

Then they shall rebuild the ancient ruins, they will raise up the former desolations, and they will repair the ruined cities, the desolation of many generations, Isaiah 61:4. *9th May 2008*

TRAMP FOR THE LORD BY CORRIE TEN BOOM

You may feel like a stranger among many who regard money, honour, and success as important issues of life. A German motto says: "What I spent, I did not have, what saved I lost, what I gave I have." And then there was painted on the corpse of a once wealthy man: Sic Transit Gloria Mundi which translated means: So Passes the Glory of this world. There are so many Glories which are tearing people from God, the Parable of Jesus with the rich man, Wealthy: one is told about the salvation of his soul, that he needs not to look at the riches, but store his riches in Christ; he says "Did Christ work it for me?" I say Who gave you the breath, strength and wisdom you have? 9th May 2008

Little Corrie one day told her father that "I am afraid I may not have the strength to be a martyr for Jesus Christ." Her father asked her "When you ask me to give you money to buy a ticket for a bus to go to Haarem, do I give it to you three weeks before?" Corrie said you give it to me the day I am going to board the bus. Her father said, "Don't you worry, when the time comes for you to be a martyr, He will give you the strength you need then."

For the wisdom of this world is foolishness with God. He is the one who catches the wise in their own craftiness, 1 Corinthians 3:19. The Lord knows the thoughts of the wise, that they are useless. So then, let no one boast in men. He captures the wise by their own shrewdness and the advice of the cunning is quickly thwarted. By day they meet with darkness and grope at noon as in the night, Job 5:13. 10th May 2008

I WAS PRAYING FOR UGANDA AFTER A DECEMBER MESSAGE by Pastor John Mulinde and the Lord had said He is going to punish Pastors, Deacons and Ushers.

Prayer, let us cry to the Lord to spare Uganda and not to punish us as we deserve. Lord, raise a man or woman to stand in the gap. We know God has you, 7,000 of us have You kept for Yourself, this You told Elijah when Jezebel was chasing him to kill him, but still one day, You looked for only one man to stand in the gap so that You would not destroy the land.

In our days He raised Bro William Seymour of Azusa Street, He raised Kathrine Khulman, she would say "O!!! The Holy Spirit is here!" then a wave would hit them and lay them on the ground, and there was Aimee McPherson - a lady revivalist who was called a Four Square Evangelist, to mention but a few, these people stood in the gap. Lord, let me stand in the gap also.

THE LORD USES WEAKER VESSELS:

Peter was a fisherman without any education, he denied You. Elijah after killing 400 false prophets of Baal was put him on the run by Jezebel. Elisha never let Gehazi take over for him but made him a leper instead of counseling him and cautioning him. Jeremiah cried I do not know how to speak and I am young, and Gideon said the clan of Manasseh is the least considered and I am the youngest.

Lord. will give You the strength when we need it at that time.

When Jesus Christ cried in the Garden of Gethsemane that My father, this Cup be taken away from me, and then he agreed and prayed Not my Will but Your Will be done, the Father gave Him the strength He needed to go the **Way** of the **Cross.** It was a peculiar Fight, a Strong man who could just say the Word and things would Work out themselves, but this time He was trampled upon, smitten, marred, crushed, crucified and said nothing. He had the **Strength** to Fight in **Silence.** Now, **Come out of him, pick up your mat and go; Now Lazarus come out.**

Jesus was arrested like a thief: "Yet He was a righteous man."

Jesus was tied with chains: "Yet he had all the power of the Word" when He said "I am He!" all fell to the ground.

Jesus was kicked, slapped, and spit upon: yet now we sing "O Hail, The Power of Jesus Name."

Jesus was made bloody mess: "Yet He is the fairest deity."

Jesus was roughed up and made vulnerably weak: "Yet now He is the strongest man who ever lived."

Jesus was made to sit in the mud: "Yet now He is sitting in Glory."

Jesus was mocked and challenged as others rolled in laughter: "Yet now all nations sing Him praises."

Jesus was displayed on the porch by Pilate: "Yet now He sits on right hand of our Father in Glory."

The crowd cried: "Crucify Him! Crucify Him!": "Yet now all races, colours and dialects Praise Him, the King of Glory."

Jesus was judged before Pilate: "Yet He is the eternal Judge for all Nations,"

Jesus was crowned with thorns: "Yet now He is crowned with Many Crowns."

Jesus was mocked and given a reed to hold: "Yet now He is holding a golden Scepter."

Jesus was clothed with a purple robe mocking Him as King: "Yet now His robe lights the whole heaven."

Jesus was stripped naked and lashed 39 stripes: "Yet by His stripes we are healed."

Jesus was displayed on the cross for all to see: "Yet every eye will see Him when He comes in Glory."

Jesus died and was buried: "Yet on the 3rd day He rose again for many will live in eternity."

Jesus was dumb founded and put to shame: "Yet now He speaks to the hearts of men and the most sought." *14th May 2008*

What can be done?

> *Turn ye even to me with all your heart, and with fasting, and with weeping, and with mourning, Blow the trumpet in Zion, sanctify*

a fast, call a solemn assembly. Then will the Lord be jealous for his land, and pity his people, And it shall come to pass afterward, that I will pour out my spirit upon all flesh; and your sons and your daughters shall prophesy, your old men shall dream dreams, your young men shall see visions, Joel 2:15 and 2:12,15,18,28

PRAYER OF VICTORY

He has made everything beautiful in its time. Also, he has put eternity into man's heart, yet so that he cannot find out what Go, has done from the beginning to the end, Ecclesiastes 3:11 (ESV).

Eternity means nothing can fill up man except his Creator, who fills heaven, earth and under world. The Creator cannot fill man unless, man's soul and spirit are prepared, expended and enlarged to receive Him, with walls broken, valleys filled, mountains leveled and barriers removed.

The Eternity can start operating in Man. "If you are in Me and Me in you if my Word is in You and you are in my Word ask or what you ask it will be given to you," John 15:7. You need to remove all the blockages as mentioned below and you will be filled with eternity.

When He is in you and you are in Him and when you pray, He will show you opened doors which have never been seen by anybody.

Message, while in California He said "I am the one who knows the biggest chunk of gold and where I placed it, no man has ever discovered it." He said He is the only one who can show it to the one he chooses. Also, He told me that there is Gold that grows in Trees no man has ever discovered it. He says He is the one who can close doors which are open and open those which are closed.

When eternity is in you, you can go where ever you want in the world within a second because you are a spirit, and when eternity becomes mature in you, you can order situations, not for personal gain, but for the glory of God and it will be so. 4th *July 2008*

When eternity is in you there is no room for self-exaltation, only Christ, He is doing everything through you, He is the Boss and you are the Foreman.

The Battle of all battles was fought in silence, He did not Fight as the world expected Him to Fight. He did not Fight in flesh and blood, but looking at them, pitying them, forgiving them: "Father, forgive them they do not know what they are doing." Also, when we are full of the eternity, when all barriers are gone, we do them good - those who do us evil, we respond with kindness. "They were going to waylay us and do harm to me and my children." They passed us, took notice of how many we were and hurried to go and plan their strategy, but on the way the Lord handled them for us. When we found them we were kind to them, we helped them and spent time with them in the Hospital, we paid for their drugs and then the Lord spoke to me: "Do you know you are treating the thugs who were going to kill you?" I shuddered but continued doing everything I could do to help them until the time when somebody else came to assist them. 9th *July 2008*

CHAPTER 7

GOD DESTINED UGANDA AS A MISSIONARY NATION

God destined Uganda as a Missionary Nation for going to all nations to preach the Gospel.

JOHN MULINDE.

BY 2000, researchers had predicted that a percentage of people would have been wiped out by AIDS and the rest would be infected, and this was going to have an impact on the economy of the nation. In 1995 Mulinde had a message from the Lord regarding 2 Chronicles 21 saying your sons will be given to slavery, already there is an indicator of a Kyeyo epidemic, young men are going to Somalia, Congo and Iraq. In 2004/5 Mulinde was in South Africa when the Lord revealed to him information about the next elections. They were going to be quite different than all other elections we have ever had due to the fact that many people were going to bombard the gates of heaven for the Lord to provide a leader.

The Lord spoke to him about the Land that has been covenanted away and there was going to be instability in the nation because Arabs and Indians were buying land. This instability meant violence. There was no power in this nation, and some people were not in their rightful places like 1 Samuel and sons of Eli. The church is bent on materialism, lies, immorality and perversion. Spiritual fathers, like God told Eli but not his sons because they started to sin; so even when the nations start to sin God tells Pastors and Prophets. Judgment, things are going to start happening. God is going to remove His hand from the ministers. There is going to be great exposure, everything was going to be uncovered, even our government leaders were going to be imprisoned, there was going to be great shame, not only in the church, but also in the nation, even the 1st family may not escape.

Dream, The Lord gave him a dream about the President. Judgment on this land and nation saying I will not finish my people who repent will come back to me. I will restore the destiny of this nation and the people are going to go out on missionary work. 29th May 2008

CHAPTER 8

WAY-LAYING GOD, TRAPPING GOD (KUTEGA MUKAMA)

ON PRAYER MOUNTAIN – Sseguku
Way-Laying God, Trapping God (Kutega Mukama)

ONE DAY ELISHA WENT ON TO SHUNEM, WHERE A WEALTHY woman lived, who urges him to eat some food. So, whenever he passed that way, he would turn in there to eat food, 2 Kings 4:8 (ESV).

The Shunamite wise woman advised her husband to build a room on the roof of their house, so that when the Man of God came he would not only eat and go but will even sleep and relax in their home so that all the blessings will remain. When the old man, Elisha was touched by the care of that family, he was moved to call the woman and ask what her wish was. So, whenever she wanted anything, i.e. if she wanted the man of God to introduce her to the king or she could walk in and he introduced her to the commander of the army.

The Prophets were greatly respected in all the land, the president may not know what was going to happen to him the next day, but the man of God would always ask the Lord to tells him what was going to happen.

WHEN I SAW AMIN FALLING FACE DOWN, WITH ALL HIS MEDALS, GOD TOLD ME "GET OUT OF HIS OFFICE."

Regarding Idi Amin, in 1978 when I saw Amin falling face down, with all his medals, God told me "Get Out of his Office."

On 27th July 1985 the Lord told me that Obote will be no more in Uganda. In 1998 Museveni left in peace. In 2000 I got the message that disaster "It is the Act of God." He said on 26th February 2014: Strike Museveni.

The Shunamite lady told him that she needed nothing, she was living among her people and was well provided for. But the Man of God still wanted this Family to be rewarded, because the lady set him a trap.

Gehazi mentioned to the man of God these people do not have a son and her husband is old. The man of God called the lady and told her that "at a time like this when I return you will be having a son" The Word of God Creates, it can never go out and come back void, when it is sent it comes back with a response, i.e. the Shunammite son, when the child was grown followed his father in the field, hurt his head, he cried and later died.

Whatever comes from God out lives, stays: "my testimony of 1986 and the soldiers of Lutwa, no one can take away what God has given you." The man of God went and brought back the boy to life, 2 Kings 8.

Elisha called the Shunammite and told her to leave the land because the Lord had told him that there was going to be a famine for 7 years, so the lady went to the Philistines and stayed there for 7 years. After 7 years the Shunammite returned.

DIVINE ENCOUNTER

The day she returned she went straight to king Jehoram to appeal for her house and land at the same time. King Jehoram had called Gehazi, the aide of Elisha, to tell him all the great things the man of God has done. Gehazi started with the Shunammite's son who was brought back to life, and there and then the Shunammite, with her son, appeared and told the story herself. The king appointed an officer to her, all that was harvested in the 7 years was to be given to her and her house be returned to her. "Whatever the thief has stolen from you, will be returned 7 times when he is caught."

Haman wanted to destroy the race of the Jews because Mordecai refused to pay respect to him. Haman was a son of Agag, the king who was killed by Prophet Samuel, (Jews) and he wanted to revenge on his father's death by killing all the Jews. The devil does not forget whatever you did to him, he will want revenge, but we can hide in the blood of Jesus. He said to his wife Zeresh and friends "even though I have been called with the king to have a banquet at the queens palace" Nothing pleases me as long as I keep seeing that Mordecai sitting at the gate.

His wife, Zeresh, told him before he goes to eat to construct a tower to hang Mordecai, and he did. At night the king did not sleep because Mordecai and Esther had a plan and went for 3 days without eating or drinking. The king asked for the records of memory, and the Holy Spirit directed him to the situation when Mordecai saved his life from a plot led by Teresh and Bigthan to assassinate the king. He asked "What was done to this man who saved my life?" They said "nothing your Excellence." He called "Who is out there?" They said Haman the Agagite is in the yard, he said Call him in here.

Guess what? He asked him; "What can be done to honour a man who pleases the king?" Haman thought that there was not any man in the land who was greater than he, so the king wanted to honour him. He started to think hard, Uhhhm ... get a crown, Uhhm ... the kingly robes, uhm ... the horse which he rides on and a high-ranking officer to go declaring where ever he passes on the road up to the city square. "This is the Man the king wants to Honour." The king told him go and do all what you have said to Mordecai the Jew. By the end of the day Haman was hanged on the gallows he had constructed for Mordecai. Esther 5 and 6.

Child of God, (Murokole) no one can understand you, as no one knows where the wind comes from and where it goes. Let your enemies laugh, rejoice, and construct the gallows to hang you; they will be hanged there themselves. Let them dig pits, set snares to catch you, bring kifaro, mahembe, and go under water. Keep praying, the Lord will turn the tables upside down for you. People in the village are backbiting and gossiping about you, keep praying, God is going to do it. *19th July 2008*

HE WHO HAS THE SON, HAS LIFE, he who does not have the Son of God does not have life. He that believeth on the Son hath everlasting life: and he that believeth not the Son shall not see life, but the wrath of God abideth on him. John 3:36 (KJV).

... take up thy bed and walk, John 5:12.

I am the resurrection and the Life. Whoever believes in me will live, even though he dies, John 11:25.

Remember you Creator in the days of youth, Eccl. 12:1.

You have no life if you have no Child and you have life if you have the Child.

Remembrance, My dear friend, what good have you done that the Lord will remember you? The Shunammite built an upper room for the man of God. She was remembered and given a son. Also her house and harvest of 7 years were returned to her.

Mordecai heard a plot to kill the king; then went and alerted the king. When a time of calamity came for him to be hanged, the Lord remembered the good thing he did, and did not let the king sleep until he caused him to see in the records of memory. Instead his enemy hanged on his own gallows he constructed.

Is the community going to remember you by your hatred? Around the block and village are you going to be remembered by stealing, drinking, taking people's wives and quarrelling? Are you still fornicating or committing adultery? When you get into trouble, what is God going to remember you by? Will he hang your enemy on his own gallows? *15th November 2008*

EARLY IN THE MORNING I TALKED TO GOD IN THE MIDST OF chaos but I was not hearing from Him. The Lord usually talked to me at length, Spirit to Spirit about my undertakings. That I am a grown up and He doesn't need to keep talking, unless He has something great to speak to me about. He said that when He keeps quiet, He is making plans for me. He talked about the Prayer of Nations, races and colours and the impact it would create in the Spirit World. That the enemy is not happy because it was like taking the bull by the horns, wishing I could see the battles angels have been Fighting for me. He said if there were to be at least ten people with that boldness this place would never be the same. He encouraged me greatly for the work I am doing, that I do not know it. He said if He were to show me what that prayer has accomplished I could not comprehend it and at the same time would cause me to be puffed up with pride and then have a great fall. He talked of Clare and that He has given her great wisdom since she turned from her rebelliousness to obedience. He showed me people who have been stealing from us. They started stealing from house to house until they reached mine. I ran to Police and reported them. The police arrested them and that was the end of the stealing. He talked about relationships which engage us and leave us without time of communion with Him; e.g. Sarah and Ivan, who I made time for these worldly relationships which took what is of God and left me empty. This went on for over an hour.

He told me:

- He has given me love over flowing.
- He has given me wisdom.
- He has given me righteousness.
- He said when He starts to do His work, we should not call it ours because we are His implementers or servants.
- Also, He said we should stop familiarizing Him, we should give Him due respect and have Holy fear for Him because He is God.
- He gave me these words: "Unto Him for the Glory of God," I wrote it on my arm twice in a trance. So, that whenever I stretch my hand I can see and say those words. 19th November 2008

KWITA OMUKAGO

Morning prayer, Lord, let me Love you!! Let me Serve you!! And may You be

My Friend. I asked the Lord (Twite Omukago) that is when one would exchange Blood on a coffee bean, friendship is sealed with the Blood. The Lord said "for me I already did, I loved man so much and gave him my Spirit." Then the Lord God formed man of dust from the ground, and breathed into his nostrils the breath of life; and man became a living soul, Genesis 2:7. God shared His Spirit with man and man lived.

Later, the thief came in Genesis 3 and lied man into rebellion, he knew what he was doing because he wanted to steal God's inheritance of mortality from him, he saw that God loved man so much and was going to take the place where he was driven. The thief does not come but to kill to steal and to destroy, John 10:10.

God, in His mercy for His friend, whom He had shared His Spirit. He chose His only begotten Son so that everyone who believes in Him may not perish. John 3:16. He had to send Jesus Christ to come and shed his blood; because we were of a great value nothing else could purchase us. He could have made a big cow and placed it in the middle of the earth and slaughtered it. He could have made it rain blood for an entire day to flood all continents of the world for the remission of sin. But it was only His blood He shared with His Spirit that was spilled to redeem mankind. The blood was to be shed to redeem friends. You are my Friends ... John 15:14, I have called you friends ... John 15:15.

CHAPTER 9

I HAVE BEEN WAITING FOR YOU TO TAKE THIS STEP

I HAVE BEEN WAITING for you to take this step. The one with a sealed Covenant Friendship, come in the house does not leave with anything; and if one with a Sealed Covenant Friendship came to your house and you let him go hungry intentionally his stomach would swell. The Lord said to Abraham in Genesis 17:11 And all shall be circumcised in the flesh of your foreskin, and it shall be the sign of the covenant between Me and you.

Behold the days are coming, declares the Lord, that I will punish all who are circumcised in the body and not in the spirit, Jeremiah 9:25 (ESV). The Lord made a sealed covenant friendship (Omukago) with Abraham. One day the Lord was passing by to go and destroy Sodom and Gomorrah, Abraham saw the Lord and asked Him do not pass me by if I have found favour in your sight, please let a little water be brought and wash your feet, rest yourselves under the tree; and I will bring a piece of bread that you may refresh yourselves and later you can go on your way.

Abraham could not let his friend pass by him, he had to give Him something to eat in his house. After a meal Abraham was escorting Him to send Him off. The Lord said "Shall I hide from

Abraham what I am about to do." A friend does not hide a secret from his covenant friend because he is more than his blood brother.

Then the Lord asked Abraham for his only son to test him and Abraham said if the Lord did not suffer me to have Isaac in my old age. I will give him to the Lord. He took him to Mount Moriah to offer him, and the Lord roared from heaven and said I have proved how much you love me Abraham do not hurt the boy.

I am a God of varieties, I do not have the same test every time, I cannot ask you to give me your son, I did that to Abraham. If I ask you to give me all your money and your vehicle, will you? I have set eternity in hearts of men yet man does not find out the work which God has done from the beginning to the end, Eccl. 3:11. I am going to do something to prove your decision.

The Word and Promises of the Lord are pure as silver fired in a furnace on the earth refined seven times, Psalm 12:6.

19*th* November 2008

CHAPTER 10

THE CALL

"I MUST NOT FORGET the power of Love." There is perfect Peace in Love, there is courage in love. There is power in Love. Many Christians for so long have been under the influence of the accuser so that it is still a part of their nature, to accuse, and it could be a while before their minds were renewed. Bro Rick Joyner said "I know that the church was still a very long way from being united." He was wondering where to begin to Unite the Church.

Wisdom replied: "You do not have to begin. It is already finished, I accomplished the Unity of My people on the Cross."

Even though it looks like the enemy has prevailed since the cross, he actually only has worked into the plan which My Father and I had from the beginning. When you preach the cross and live by its power, you will do my will. Those who serve Me and not their own ambitions will soon recognize one another and be joined together.

Those who have the true fear of God do not have to fear anything on the earth. As you behold me you will not fear. **Those who have the true fear of God do not have to**

fear anything on the earth. If you fear, it is because you are not beholding me.

When the evil in mankind has become full united with the evil one, the great time of trouble will come upon the earth, Rev. 22:10. Then all of mankind and the whole creation will understand the futility and tragedy of rebellion. People have become lovers of themselves with escalation of immorality worldwide. Gay activities, pornography, homosexuals, ritual killings, defilements, incest, etc. At the same time, my people will become fully united with me, and My great light will stand against the great darkness.

Those who walk in lawlessness will fall into the deep darkness. Those who walk in obedience will shine forth as the stars of heaven. Humility and obedience will always lead to Me. As you come to Me, you will behold and manifest My Glory. The heavens and the earth are about to behold the difference between the light and the darkness. You are called to live between the darkness and the light in order to call those who live in darkness to the light. Even now I do not desire for any to perish.

If all of mankind could just have a glimpse of Your Judgment Seat, they would all quickly repent. Then Jesus said I will reveal Myself. When evil has run its full course, then I will show Myself to the World. As the evil one is being revealed through fallen men, I will be revealed through restored men. The Lord will reveal His nature in His people. People should love the Lord and the truth but not the glory and power.

Those who choose to obey when the whole world is disobeying are worthy to be heirs with Me. These will be worthy to rule with Me, to see My glory, and to share it. These are the ones who do not live for themselves, but for me. Some of the greatest of these brethren of mine are about to be revealed. They will stand for truth against the greatest darkness. They will remain steadfast through the greatest trials. I have brought you here, and I am sending you back to encourage them to stand and not faint for the time of their salvation is near.

Satan saw the glory of My Father and beheld the myriads who served Him, yet he still fell. He fell because he started to trust in the glory and power that the Father had shared with him instead of trusting the Father. Those who will be entrusted with the power and glory I share with them in these times must not put their trust in the power of glory, but in Me. True faith is never in yourself, your wisdom or the power that I have given to you. True faith is in Me.

As you grow in the true faith that is in Me, you will grow in dependence on Me, and you will trust yourself less. Those who begin to trust in themselves will not be able to carry the weight of my power or glory, they can fall just as the evil one did. My strength is made perfect in weakness, but you must never forget that in yourself you are weak, and by yourself you are foolish.

The angels marvel when suffering men and women who have beheld so little of the glory here remain steadfast for Me and My truth in times of darkness. These are worthy to be called my brethren and to be called the sons and daughters of My Father. On earth, the truth often looks weak and easily defeated. My truth and My goodness will prevail for all of eternity, and so will all who come to Me because they love the truth. These will shine forth as the stars which were made in Honour of him.

STAY AWAY FROM THE PEOPLE AND THINGS THAT MAKE YOU LOSE YOUR VISION.

Stay away from the people and things that make you lose your vision. When we get to the place of our ultimate vision, we will not judge people by the colour of their skin, gender or age. We will not judge others by appearances, but after the spirit. You must keep going for as far as you can see. Never stop as long as you can still see further. If you do not use your vision by walking in what you see, you will lose it and perish. 19th *November 2008*

GOD NEVER USES A MAN GREATLY UNTIL HE HURTS HIM DEEPLY!!!

Abraham was told he had to leave his own people and go to a foreign land.

Jacob had wrestled with God and was cheated by his uncle Laban.

Joseph was sold into slavery by his brothers and persecuted by Potiphar's wife.

Job was allowed to go through many trials for 7 years.

David was persecuted by king Saul.

Mordecai was persecuted by Haman.

Jeremiah was thrown into the pit by king Zedekiah for giving true prophecy.

Elijah was persecuted by Jezebel for killing all her false prophets.

Micaiah was imprisoned in a Joash prison by king Ahab for telling the truth. 12th *December 2008*

SEMINAR: INTRODUCTION AND PURPOSE

This series of seminars started in 2004 after the Lord put it on my heart and I joined members of Tooro Intercessors. Daisy Birungi, Vicent Alijuna and Robert Rutafa used to come and meet to pray in my office at Amber House Kampala. Later I introduced to them a burden God had put on my heart to go back home to lift our people.

The Seminars stopped for some time in 2005 when Robert Rutafa was murdered in May 2005 and resumed in 2006 through 2008 when we conducted many seminars, film shows and visited about 10 churches in Mwenge North area.

PLACE NYAMABUGA

Place: Nyamabuga, this name means the Place of many Springs of Healing Waters. This came about in the era of the Tooro Kingdom. There used to be Embuga Water Springs belonging to the king of Tooro which he had passed on to his Relative of Bagweri Clan. In 1930 the cows died after being vaccinated by the British. All the cattle keepers of Tooro Kingdom and Bunyoro Kitara, used to bring their cows to drink at Embuga so that their cows would get healed of diseases. Also, they found that there were some minerals which were causing these waters to boil so they sealed the well. So that is where the name of Nyamabuga came from; but now this place is going to become Springs of Healing Waters for the people of God.

PURPOSE OF THE SEMINAR

God sent His only begotten Son to die in our place, so that we may live, John 3:16.

As we are gathered here, God has a plan for us and has purposed each one of us to be of a great value for His kingdom. The people who know their God will do great exploits, display great strength and take actions, Daniel 11:32. That is why we are coming to inform you early, so that you do not fall into the same traps we have seen people falling into in other parts of the world. The devil which is in US, Europe, Asia, and Africa is the same;

except he changes coats according to the level of education, income, colour and race of the people. Therefore: "well warned is well armed" (Embulirire tefa yoona or Akuhabura omuhanda). $21^{st} - 24^{th}$ January 2009

THIS IS THE JUDGMENT, THAT THE LIGHT HAS COME INTO the world and men loved the darkness rather than the light, for their deeds were evil. For everyone who does evil hates the light, and does not come to the Light for fear that his deeds will be exposed. But he who practices the truth comes to the light, so that his deeds may be manifested as having wrought of God, John 3:19.

- Servants of God are crashing their own vehicles making Self-accidents.
- Doctrines are copying other ministries order of doing things.
- Missions are joining churches with wrong doctrines and ideologies, i.e. Kimera, Biraro who went to US and came back with a cultish doctrine from India.
- Rebellion has created Self-styled pastors who are self-appointing and they are not listening to messengers of God, e.g. redeeming experience, lying and unfaithfulness.
- Competition for worldly riches and not focused on heaven saying they want their inheritance now, now and here, e.g. end of year festivals.
- Greedy spirits that are leading them to acquire false riches by hooks or crooks. Some have become gay homosexuals, have joined satanic clubs, are preaching to say aggressive prayers, they want visas,

Other pastors have marriages to attract young believers.
- Possessions become so important they take church and people of God as their property.
- No time for saving souls getting busier and busier and without no time to listen and talk with their Creator. They are on call 24hrs and people who need counsel no need to have made appointments to see them.

SALVATION WHICH IS TAKING TO HEAVEN IS OF A TOTAL MAN:

- the way you live – clean environment
- the way you dress – proper dress
- the way you talk – to your family and others
- the way you eat – food is a big issue to people of God

Lastly some of you have already fallen into the trap of the old prophet, he knew he was no longer effective, yet he persuaded the prophet who was sent to curse, the altar of Jeroboam. After cursing the altar the old prophet had trapped him into disobedience. God had commanded him not to eat or come back on the same road - your backsliding friends who know they are not heaven bound but know you have valuable things in your hands; they want to see that you lose it. Also, you do not make them feel guilty. They will call you names, serious ones, even at times and tell others that you have a cult trying to spoil you. If they fail, they will try to befriend you and tell you they are also saved, I am also a Man of God, come with me, have something to eat. Ah! Ah! Be careful they want you to perish with them. Sugar illustration. 21st - 24th *January 2009*

Rev Agnes I Numer and Gertrude Kabatalemwa

CHAPTER 11

YOU ARE AN ORIGINAL

You're Born an Original, Do not Die a Copy. John L. Mason.

MAN IS the only creature that refuses to be what he is. Do not just look for miracles because you are a miracle and you are wonderfully made, Psalm 139:14.

One of the hardest things about climbing the ladder of success is getting through the crowd of copies at the bottom. You are not created to be all things to all people. More than 90% of all flowers have either an unpleasant odor or none at all. Yet the flowers with the sweetest fragrance are the ones that we most remember.

Following the easy path of least resistance is what makes men and rivers crooked, there are people looking to get easy, ill-gotten success.

Do not copy the behaviours of this world, but be a new and different person with a fresh newness in all that you do and think.

Then you will learn from your own experience how His ways will really satisfy you, Romans 12:2

There are many things that catch my eye, but there are only a very few that catch my heart, those I consider worthy to pursue. 11th February 2009

ABOUT FEAR

The great evangelist Billy Sunday once said, "Fear knocked at my door. Faith answered and there was no one there."

Many people are so filled with fear that they are running through life from something that isn't after them. Fear of the future is a waste of the present. My childhood fear was of lions. Worry is a sister of fear and they walk together. Worry is like a rocking chair, it keeps you going, but you do not get anywhere. Every morning I spend fifteen minutes filling my mind full of God, so, there is no room left over for worry thoughts.

It always costs more not to do God's Will than to do it." Thus you spend much time running around or trotting the globe, spending your time, energy, money, etc. but when you do the Will of God you save time, money and energy.

Dissatisfaction and discouragement are not the absence of things, but the absence of a clear vision.

When you are an original and walk in God's plan, you shine like a star in the firmament. Copying is the darkness where the originals float.

No wind blows in favour of a ship without a destination. Always, trials come your way because you are heading somewhere, where negative forces do not want you reach. If you have no destination expect no winds trying to stop you. A person without a conviction is like a ship without a rudder. *14th February 2009*

A YOUNG WOMAN POISONED HERSELF, THIS WAS THE THIRD time. That night we were in a prayer vigil interceding until the Lord delivered her. The men had to get her in a taxi. On their arrival I woke up to pray and this is the message I got:

ON THE KNEES.

> *On the knees is the proper Posture for sowing the Seed. A Christian on their knees see more than kings, presidents, wisemen, and rich men of the world than others on their tiptoes.*

Before our Lord went for that eventful journey to redeem mankind, He went on His knees in the Garden of Gethsemane and sowed the seed which was to carry Him over that excruciating agony. When they said "We are looking for Jesus of Nazareth" and He said I am He!! They reeled back and fell on the ground, He found He was still possessing the Power. He had to swallow it up, and give Himself to His enemy.

The seed He sowed on His knees enabled Him to accept all the accusations, the kicking, the pulling off His beard, the spitting on Him, people putting on Him a purple robe and mocking Him, stripping Him naked and then flogging Him. He fell under the heavy cross so many times and finally, the crucifixion.

The Pharisees, the Sadducees and Sanhedrin's, on their tiptoes, could not see much what our Lord was seeing on His

Knees, He said "Not my Will, but Thy Will be done." Or else they would not have crucified the King of Glory. They did not go on their knees first when they started to look for ways to accuse Him falsely.

On His knees He saw You and Me and saw all what we were going through in the toucher chambers of the devil, He saw us in furnaces, in fire places, in lion's dens, in snakes' snares, in pits of mire and chained in prisons. All this He saw and said Father Not my Will.

On His knees He saw the repented thief on the cross and told him Today, we will be together in Paradise. On His knees He knew He was to forgive His enemies because they did not know what they were doing, otherwise they were going to perish in their sins.

On His knees He said "It is finished." He saw the power of the grave where the devil held His people at ransom, and He paid the ransom with His blood. "They overcame him with the blood of the lamb and the Word of their testimony." Rev. 12:11.

On our knees, now, we also should get on our knees and sow the seed. The Kingdom of heaven will hear us when we call, poison will be neutralized, turn around healing for accident victims, the noose of suicide ropes will be stopped, demons will flee, captives will be set free from prison walls of false religions.

Let us go on our knees when the spear, machete, club waiving gangs come to attack and we will paralyze them because we have seen far.

On our knees, when people do not go on their knees, but stand on their tiptoes, they see nothing and resort to Fight in flesh and blood in carnality. The battle on the knees is spiritual, only those in the spirit see it. If you are in the flesh you crash yourself and you cannot fast and pray. You get ulcers and you faint because you are not in spirit.

Kings in Palaces, presidents in State Houses, rich-men in

Mansions and wise-men in castles on their tiptoes cannot see what a tea plucker or herdsman who has never seen a blackboard can see when he is on his knees. *18th February 2009*

> *Message: Isaiah 53, Isaiah 5*
> *Song: I call upon the Lord, who is worthy to be*
> *praised, and I am saved from my enemies.*
> *The Lord liveth and blessed be my rock; and*
> *exalted be the God of my salvation.*
> *Psalm 18:3; God is my fortress. Psalm 46. 27th*
> *February 2009*

MY LIFE IS LIKE A VEHICLE, I AM THE DRIVER, THE ROAD IS ROUGH TO HEAVEN.

My life is like a vehicle, I am the driver, the road is rough to heaven. It's full of potholes, floods, cattle, boda-boda, taxi and drunkards driving on the road.

I need to be sober. There are fires where schools are being burnt and one of the worst fires was in April 2008 killing 20 small girls in a girl's dormitory called the Owino Fire on 25th February 2009, and beheading children is getting worse.

The young woman who took strong rat poison, I had a two day fast and the Lord delivered her. On the 28th retiring to bed after prayers. I got a call from the village that she was almost to the point of death. Life is full of experience. *28th February 2009*

Message, Jesus and a pharisee named Nicodemus, John 3:1-7; Therefore, if anyone is in Christ, he is a new creation. The old has passed away, 2 Corinthians 5:17.

IN THE OFFICE, SHARING WITH ONE MEMBER WHO WAS complaining of pains and confessing to be Saved I gave him this message:

People are Saved but Not Born Again. We find there are so many people walking saved but still living in sin without any change in their lives. They lie, fornicate, steal, hate etc. Every Born-Again believer should be baptized in water. This isn't in order to be saved, but rather because you have been saved, Romans 6:3-4. Do you know that all of us who have been baptized into Christ Jesus have been baptized into His Death?

Therefore, we have been buried with Him through baptism into death, so that as Christ was raised from the dead through the glory of the father, so we too might walk in newness of life, Born Again, 2 Corinthians 5:17 says we are New Creatures. Water baptism symbolizes your baptism into the Body of Christ, you become part of His Eternal Body. He put eternity into our soul so that no man can find out the work which God maketh from the beginning even to the end, Eccl. 3:11. There is one body, and one spirit, even as ye are called in one hope of your calling; one Lord, one faith, one Baptism, one God and Father of all, who is above all, and through all, and in you all, Ephesians 4:4-6.

We need to get Born Again, that is when a fundamental change comes in our lives. Jesus Christ told Nicodemus "You must be born again." Unless one is born again he cannot see the kingdom of God. In the name of salvation; saved people are doing every sin under the sun and yet sitting in churches. One can be in the Born Again Church and be saved and still not Born Again. That is why we are hearing pastors are gays, homosexuals, fornicators, thieves, etc.

Who is Born Again? Therefore if anyone is in Christ, he is a new creature, old things are passed away; behold, all things are become new, 2 Corinthians 5:17. There is conviction of sin within you. There is a gong which rings a warning whenever you are sinning or have sinned and the sun can never go down without you knowing that you have sinned.

Being Born Again gives a two-way communication between man and his God talking listening to the Father, and the Father talking and Listening to His new child. In being Born Again there is seeking and searching for a closer encounter with the creator and there is Great Hunger.

In Saved Life, many people have no experience of a Talking God and wonders whether He talks; and they are surprised when they hear that God talks. Chicago Pastor in Baptist Church comes to Uganda every year to listen to stories of How God talks to people. You can see the expression on his face when listening to my stories.

They say Gertrude has many stories, they call them "stories," yet these are life giving stories. In 1984 the Lord showed me the manner which 4 American Journalists were going to be executed in the Middle East. Another time He showed me a child who had taken poison, and He instructed me to go to pray for him at Mengo Hospital.

When you accept Jesus Christ immediately you receive salvation. You have to move further or deeper. This is like going to a Hospital or Clinic, you pass beyond the sign post (Mulago Hospital) and go inside to look for a Doctor to examine you and give you a prescription for medicine to cure your ailment.

When we get saved, we come with many diseases which need Dr Holy Spirit to identify and give us the right prescription.

Passing the sign post is one step of being "Saved." Making efforts to move further inside the Hospital and look for the Doctor is an act of seeking and yearning for more than the Sign Post of Salvation. Looking for Dr Jesus, and when you find Dr Jesus, He will Listen to your heart beat, touch here or there and Diagnose or identify what is troubling you. He can give you a Prescription for your cure. You went to Hospital sick and came out healed. Therefore if anyone is in Christ, he is a new creature: old things are passed away; behold, all things are become new, 2 Corinthains 5:17.

CHAPTER 12

BONDAGES AND PRISON

COVENANTS: WHAT IS A COVENANT?

IT IS something that looks like an irrevocable commitment and it is like a chain binding two people together. The chain will always be dragging the partners along. Covenants may come through inheritance of parents, grandparents or ancestors. You can enter into a bad covenant by decision of your own for safety reasons, some join a secret society for protection. You may join to become wealthy through covenants with the devil. People make covenants by drinking each one's blood (omukago).

Produced out of covenants are curses, bondages, and yokes.

BONDAGES AND PRISON

Many people are born in bonded or imprisoned families. These yokes are prison walls that need to be broken when you are in an Inner Circle of people deeply seeking and searching for the Lord. You cannot break the covenant's yoke, that your great, great grands have made with the devil with Just Acceptance of Christ, you need to take another step and be Born-Again in order break the yoke.

> ... and it shall come to pass when thou shalt have the dominion, that thou shalt break his yoke from off thy neck, Genesis 27:40.

There are so many ways of being yoked, self-made yokes because you could have yoked yourself by covenants, contracts, or agreements you made by getting involved with witchcraft, cannibalism, idolatry, etc. by making promises you forgot to considering first, e.g. a girl or a boy making a promise "if you will leave me, I will kill myself." The enemy is always listening. The day comes as one leaves, straight away the demon of death comes and says kill yourself. One day a lady cut her own throat because a man had left her.

Marriage yokes, when men are marrying women who are from pagan families and are already hooked (embandwa za Kaikara, Mulindwa, abarongo), where rituals were observed (ebigunguza, ndyoka ya bakonjo, nyabiingi) and other bondages. When a man married a woman who is hooked to satan he also became part of that party. When she wants you to buy meat to for feasting with the idols and you have to obey or if the husband asks the wife to prepare a meal for the idols you cannot say no, so you both become a part of the idol worshipers, 1 Corinthians 10:25-32.

Sexual yokes, Men or women getting involved in sex with same sex or young boys and girls who are having satanic involvements. The Lord warns His people that: Believers should not be yoked with non-believers. When you are only saved and you are not born again it is easy to be lured in sexual immorality with unbelievers. The Word says Do not you not know that your bodies are members of Christ? 1 Corinthians 6:15-18. Or do you not know that the one who joins himself to a prostitute is one body with her? The two shall be one body so flee fornication. Do not you know that your body is the temple of the Holy Spirit who is in you? For you have been bought with a price; therefore, glorify God in your body, and in your spirit, which are God's. The one who joins himself to the Lord is one spirit with him. Also, do not be yoked with non-believers. Some men and women are agents of satan, once you join your body together with them it gives an open door for the devil's agents to enter you through a sex door. Some unbelievers use witchcraft to hook partners so that they do not leave them.

Incest yokes, when blood brothers and sisters commit fornication together, they form covenants. If a woman has ever been involved in this type of incest, the end will be in a broken home and children will not be fruitful. I know one of my relatives married his daughter, they produced beautiful 9 children, girls and boys. One very beautiful girl was going to marry the king but she died mysteriously.

Friend's yokes, walking with friends who may lead you into traps like smoking, Njahi, Mairungi, drinking alcohol, seeing movies of sex, violence, or witchcraft. There is a movie of Harry Potter which has introduced many youth to witchcraft etc.

Ancestral yokes, bondages from ancestral yokes of fathers, mothers, uncles and aunties that when they die want you to continue with their duties, they used to perform in devil worshiping. Inheriting meaningless or idolatrous names, which start affecting your life; Ntogota give birth to Alifaijo, Alifaijo gives birth to Kahigwa, (Byakunaga, Kazibona, Kadoma, Kahinde-Otafire Kyomya, Mulindwa, Rwakaikara). They left inherited to you witchcraft and idolatry, even the regalia they used to wear perform the rituals, e.g. cowries crowns (seashells), offertory baskets, costumes, spears, shrines, eating and drinking vessels, etc. are owned by you now.

Partaking food offered to idols, eating food offered to idols. There are two different ways to eat food sacrificed to idols. ONE way is to actually partake during the sacrifice ritual in which the eater is giving honor and worship to the idol. The SECOND way is to eat food of which a portion was first sacrificed to an idol, but the eating is separate from the sacrifice and not a part of the worship or giving of honour to the idol. Like now all the meat bought in the markets was once the animals slaughtered by Moslem's rituals, who face the animal to Mecca. By eating this meat bought from the market, you are not participating in the ritual sacrificed in any way. That is why you have to pray for any meal put before you. In some homes the first portion of every meal each day is laid before a statue of an idol as a form of sacrifice to that idol. Some satanists give offering to the ground before they eat or drink anything.

Cursed/occultic places, visiting friends at places like going to attend Moslem festivals, funeral rituals, or watch procession of witches, idolatry Match or procession of Barongo dance. To go to sites of kings' burial places, caves, shrines, Ancestral sites, Occultic places Cleopatra or the pyramids in Egypt; i.e. one day a lady who belonged to our church in 1980s went to Hoima to for a crusade, after they visited a witch doctor's home who had a shrine she went into a shrine, got hold of one of the ritual sticks, and broke it. As she was breaking it, she heard it breaking her back bone, and that was her beginning of trouble. She was brought to Kampala straight and taken to Mulago Hospital, she could not walk again and she could not stand again. She spent a long time in hospital.

Gifts from occultic people, people may give you gifts like of some sort or money and when you accept it, a curse of poverty or destruction is activated in your life. Occultic people may pretend to sell you something like an object specifically for use in satan's service as an attachment to get your money. Anoint the object and cleanse it in the name of Jesus, the curse will be broken off it. Refuse gifts from people you do not know well who mean good to you.

Curses from God, parents, kings, witches and others, a curse from God, one can cause himself a curse from God by disobedience, e.g. you know all what you did in the past and instead of repenting you go and join a church which has no power to point at sin, or you join a false doctrine or cult to cover up your past. You remain there as if nothing is happening. You cause yourself a God's curse.

Parent's curses, if one gets involved in Fighting, quarreling or any other involvement which may cause a parent to say unpleasant statements towards you, e.g. "You will never speak before me and be heard," Also, "your children, and children of your children, will beat you as you have beaten me." That is, it, one will suffer in life because they will never make any advancement.

King's curses, if a king curses you it is a strong curse. One day an old man I know who was keeping the king's royal cattle at home. He took a bull the king loved so much, killed it and ate it. When the king came and asked for his prize bull it was nowhere. He cursed the old man that he will not have any more cattle, he did have herds and herds of cattle, but they all died, and died drinking water.

Witch's curse, one may go to witches and make agreements for a sacrifice then fail to take it as agreed, a witch doctor can utter a curse from his demons.

Curses from others like friends, relatives, even strangers, if one may fail to fulfill a promise or fail to give help at a time needed, i.e. one may be dying and wants to eat or drink something and you refuse to give it to them when you have it. A dying man may leave you a curse, (Tyera!!! Biisi!!!!).

Marriage bondages, one is born in a family with a chain of witchcraft, she gets married to a family of night dancers or idolatry. Chain meet, and make a blend, mix and when they get children, they have double bondage even if one studies up to the level of the highest education, still that devil will strike at any time he wants to strike, because he stores his victim. I had influential relatives who were held in high esteem in the society, to the extent of owning jet planes. A county chief, one of the Crown Bearers in the Palace, married to influential High clans, one of my 2 aunties. who were also from a devil worshiper of the kingly clan. He fathered more than 15 children, whose studies made them High Ranking officers in the army, teachers, managers, air hostesses, and jet owners. When they used to assemble one would say "even if heaven has to come down, this family will never even smell of poverty or suffering."

The devil stores snares and traps of the ancestors and waits for a victim in that family. Someone whom it will close in the web. That is why you have to be Born Again, in order to set your spiritual, long, range binoculars and telescopes and pull out the devil's traps and snares that he set so long ago through your ancestors.

This family of my relatives time came as one by one, starting with the old man, wives remained to see how all the children were going to start dropping, accidents, AIDS, tumors, the man with jets who lived in Switzerland just dropped dead, others started dropping dead, one was in a plane and she just died just there, then the old women also followed. Whenever people went to bury if it rained there was nowhere to take shelter, even with all those riches which used to flow like a river, nothing was done at home.

Mansions were built in London, Zurich, and Paris but not

even a hut at home. When there is an ancestor trap, snare bondages in the family when one wants to break off by accepting Jesus and go to the right church where one would be told how to set spiritual binoculars and telescopes to see where the cause of the matter was. The devil leads them to occultic shrines, wrong doctrine teaching churches, i.e. one man who was so involved in killings that the whole family was having bad reputation in killings and torturers as this family was involved in murderous political parties. Trying to escape revenge one joined a theological college and became a Clergyman to keep away his enemies. This does not work, one needs to repent and clean up all the dirt, still this kept him in bondage and keeps the whole family in a joint prison.

Victims and children, people in joint bondage cannot have meaningful children. They may get still births, abortions, or miscarriages every time the wife conceives, She gets still birth or series of miscarriages. These miscarriages are as sacrifices to ancestral covenants made many years ago. At times you find family gives birth to children who are deformed, handicapped or give birth to objects, stones, rivers, or snakes. Other children die young or are born with contaminated blood cells. Some are born with inherited incurable diseases like asthma, cancer, or fits. When they grow old, they die an abrupt death or through diseases like AIDS that can kill all the grownup children of the family as father and mother remain childless. At times, others when they reach an important goal on the eve of their study or eve of their wedding they die, or run mad because they had so much wisdom, yet it is the evil one.

Harvesting, this is when a family goes on and enjoys all the good times, children are grown, graduate, have marriages get good jobs. You find all the children are well off, then what they need to do is help their parents up to a certain age before they start dying one, after another, like the family of my relatives above. People start dying left and right without a good cause of death. At times going or coming from burial you hear that the family of five all died in a car accident.

Strangers will enjoy your riches, you are saved even when you become rich. Either you may have decided to go and live in London or America, there you may prosper, have houses, money etc. while our family will be grassing, living in poverty, going for prayers for you to remember coming back to help them. I had a Pastor in my church who left for America, and left his wife behind; later she also looked for a ticket and followed him; who left all the children including young twins by themselves. All the children grew but some started misbehaving because there was nobody to care for them.

Poverty, families due to ancestral bondages and covenants they made, children may follow in poverty of the family. Famine in the family, one will work so hard, but achieve nothing even the food he grows in the garden will yield little, to the extent that they always will be spending money to buy food for the family. When he tries to break the seal that covenant of poverty curses will come in any form, e.g. fire and burn whatever stock one has in a shop, market, fire can come for only you but leaves others victims, yet it was after only you. If you break the yoke and survive just for a period before Lightning may come and kill your animals all at one hand. You try hard and stock your shop and furnish your house, then thieves will come once and carry everything away and you go back to zero. At other times, you will think everyone is bewitching you and whatever you have you take it to witch doctors to buy mahembe. And they will take all your money until when you get poor because everything you got witch doctors tell you they want it.

Encounters (Orugwiso), the day you get your salary or money, that is when you fall sick, that is when you meet with thieves and they take all the money, that is when a child, wife, mother, or father gets very sick and needs immediate treatment or that is when you are called to go to the village where your house has caught fire or somebody has accused you and you are to go to court. Problems wait for you until when you get your pay and they surface. When you are called for a job, the moment you reach there someone else has just been there before you, if you get it after one month you get very sick by the time you come back it is taken.

SEVERAL SOURCES OR ROOTS OF BONDAGE AND CURSES EXIST.

Inheritance, the sins of the forefathers committed while still living, e.g. witch craft, idolatry, cannibalism, satan worshiping, or covenants, agreements, contracts they made with satan.

Broken dedication to satan, if you break dedication of what you used to give satan, if you stop giving respect you used to give to the devil, that is breaking your dedication.

Ancestors acceptance of bondage or curses on the lives of descendants, this is in the case of the Jews, when they killed Jesus, they said "let His blood be on us and our grandchildren." Even if they are no longer living parents, or grandparents may swear that their children and grandchildren will continue with devil or satanic rituals.

Involvement with unclean and unholy things, this is when one plays with unholy, one can go and get witchcraft left for a different purpose and you start playing with it. When we were young a neighbour shifted and left behind all her fetishes in the house. The young children went to search in the empty house and one found one horn they used in idolatry. It stuck on the hand of the boy, other children fought hard but removed it from him. All the children got scared of that incident.

THERE IS A PROCESS TO SET YOURSELF FREE FROM SATANIC COVENANTS.

Past History, get all the information concerning your ancestors, grandparents, parents and all your past involvement of any kind you know which could have opened a door for bondage. If you do not have any one to tell you take time to pray and fast, ask the Holy Spirit, He will reveal it to you. Your ignorance cannot exempt you, because the evil one is looking where he can hook you, and ignorance is the best way, he is killing his victims.

Repentance, you need to repent from whatever sins you have committed consciously and unconsciously, every sin you do is done against God.

Identify, know and say the particular covenants you are breaking. There are different types of covenants, bondages, agreements to break like inter-marriage covenants, covenants of death exchange e.g. cannibalism, blood covenants (Omukago).

Be specific, use the Word of God as the basis of your spiritual warfare. Just as everything positive was created by the Word, so everything negative can be destroyed by the invocation of the Word.

Be systematic, concentrate on breaking covenants before moving on to curses, because curses are results of covenants. Covenants are Agreements made and curses are the Products of these agreements. Covenants must be Broken before the curses are broken.

Be aggressive, pray with determination, steadfast, bold and be resolute. Believe in the power of the Word of God in your mouth to nullify whatever agreements that satan holds against you.

Be spontaneous, deal with whatever the Holy Spirit drops in your heart that you may not have been aware of, the Holy Spirit can lead you to deal away covenants you did not know of, i.e. in my early time of salvation in dreams the Holy Spirit used to bring me snakes, then centipedes as big and as long as a train. And those were my ancestral snake demons they used to worship. I continued breaking those ancestral covenants.

When you are still under the bondage, bad things happen to you. There is no any amount of fasting and prayer, confession and speaking in tongues that can release the person from under an evil covenant if the person does not stand his/her ground and disentangle themselves. You will always confess you are saved but not living a life of breakthrough in so many areas.

CHAPTER 13
DEEP WELL OF MY HEART

AS I PRAYED, I felt that I have no words in a human language which can express the real meaning from deep in my heart. So I pleaded the Holy Spirit to interpret and give the real meaning in the understandable heavenly language of my Thanksgiving and Love towards the Lord.

I remembered the scripture which says The heart of man is deep No one can understand it. Then I said to the Lord, please, it is you who have that vessel which you can send and draw the real meaning of my Thanksgiving and Love, the real meaning from the deep well of my heart.

At this note the Lord brought me a Scene at the Well of Sychar in John 4. I saw the Lord sitting on the well of Sychar and as she drew the water. Our Lord asked her for drink, because He did not have something to draw the water with. She asked Him how He could ask water to drink from a despised person who was regarded as low class.

Therefore, we need someone with a container to draw the water from the deep human well. 27th *March 2009*

CHAPTER 14

CONFERENCE OF YOUTHFUL MARRIED COUPLES

BY NYAMABUGA BORN Again Church

HOW ONE CAN BE A YOUTH/MARRIED AND STILL LIVE A CHRISTIAN BREAKTHROUGH LIFE?

INTRODUCTION:

- We hope to get more of this kind because we are not going to keep preaching to you, some of you have gone through experience and God has ever used you more, but the things of God are always New. He talks at different times to different people in the same message but in a different way.
- We have been calling you on many Seminars and Crusades but this time we said we should change and bring you Conference/Workshop in order to teach the youth and married couples. This I saw was

needed in the last Seminar when one of the ladies stood to speak, she tackled many areas which left me speechless. Many women were touched by what she shared but it was only a cup from the ocean, so I was motivated to see that we get her to pour her experience out for three days to our women and our future to be women.

- Therefore, I said not only ladies should benefit, but also our gentlemen should not be left behind, we have dynamic men of God to give their experience in every area at home, outside and in the Church because many people have been pointing fingers at us "that one also is called." In this area Christians in Born-Again Churches need teaching in order to Walk right with God and keep their integrity and walk with their heads up.
- However, we beg you when we call you, for these meetings sit and settle down, there is something the Lord wants to teach you, do not have that divided mind of what is happening at home, because we give you invitations. In time you see that plan for your home for the three days you will be away. Because even us, we leave all our business in the hands of the Lord to come and be a blessing to you.
- Most of you here if I am not mistaken, are not having time to read the Word as it is required or read Christian literature of Great men and women God used in the 18th to this Century for World Revival. Because you have no time or money, to buy these books, therefore, we get this information (kubasakira) in order to come and warn you, where these men and women made it or failed so that you are aware and that you do not fall in the same traps.

So please when we call you come ready to receive what God has for you in store.

2ND LESSON YOUTH

You're Born an Original Don't DIE a COPY

JOHN L. MANSION

MAN IS THE ONLY CREATURE THAT REFUSES TO BE WHAT HE IS.

YOUTH DO NOT COPY FOREIGN CULTURES.

Many youths have copied fashions and fads; these days communication systems go very fast in a matter of a few hours on the Internet cafes. You shall not fall in with the many to do evil, Exodus 23:2 says you shall not follow a crowd to do evil. Beloved, do not imitate what is evil, but what is good, 3 John 1:11. Be informed that most fads originate in witchcraft, some come from rock music stars and through Hollywood.

Fads of clothing, many articles of clothing and jewelry have occultic designs, pictures and symbols of them, many on shirts, e.g. hell with flames of fire, dragons, signs of pirates, devils, snakes, or skeleton dripping blood, etc. demon spirits can legally attach to these items. Anyone wearing these comes directly under a curse. Some elite authorities have had to ban the kids from wearing T-shirts because of the rebellion they display.

Vision of Pastor Mulinde: The Word of God says women should not wear men's dressing, and men not women's dressing. Men putting on necklaces for women. Women putting on trousers that is disobedience or rebellion. You may not go to hell because of putting on trousers, but you may lose some marks or stars on your crown. Many women's clothing are designed by underworld to entice men; be careful of what you put on, e.g. Kundi show, G-String, backless, micro-mini, hot pants, etc. A revelation the Lord gave a lady, "How are you dressed is the way you arrive in heaven?" Suppose when you get there you will be having on a wig of human hair on your head; and you are in trousers yet the scripture is there which tell you not to put on men's clothing.

Hair, perming and wet-look first came to USA in the late 70s and spread in Africa, now it became a norm and everybody has to perm her hair, to the extent that even women if the husband does not give her money for perming can divorce. You think beauty is from the hair? The Lord is saying let your beauty come from inside, 1 Peter 3:3. Hair Plaiting and wigs, be careful, the enemy is not sleeping, he is looking for all the ways to see that he destroys you by bringing to you things which you do not even consider that can affect your Christian walk. At first people used to plait hair with their own hair. I plaited hair more than all of you here just using my own hair and I used to look like a Goan. People used to wonder whether that was my hair or not. Then the enemy brought braids and wigs of human air to the factory.

By using human hair and wigs you do not know who sold that hair you have put on your head and the head is the most important part of your body, that is where God put the brain, control tower. If you wear the wig or human hair of a prostitute in Thailand you may start getting demons sleeping with you in dreams, dreams of being raped, etc. In case you buy a wig or plait, your hair mixed with human hair of a poor woman who may have lived in abject poverty in Cambodia or Korea who sold her hair for one reason or another. Sister you will carry the covenants that person's family, or person may have made, which may result in suffering the bondage of prostitution or poverty curses.

Because on your head you are carrying a spirit of another person on your head, hands may be laid on you, if you do not recognize and break that spirit or throw it away your breakthrough will be limited.

Pig's tail, fool's tail, goat's tail hair, Bible warns us you shall not shave around the side of head, nor shall you disfigure the edges of your beard, Leviticus 19:26-28. Barbers after shaving people hair off without their permission they cut the corners of their heads whether boys or girls. I asked one of the children at home why she was shaving the sides of her head to disfigure her like that, she said the barber does it on his own. There are so many people now working on instructions of the devil.

Boys in the 1990s were cutting their hair and leaving one small bunch of hair long in the middle of the back which looks like a tail; this demonic Fad started in England by some rock-music performers who were also involved in a witchcraft group called wicca. The tails are actually called a goat's tail and is a sign of allegiance to satan who is always represented by the goat. Christians take their children and cut this sign in their heads. That is where we trace the beginning of his rebellion back to when he starts wearing this style.

In ancient Rome and Greece men shaved sides of their heads and also sculpted designs and strips into the hair on the sides of their heads as a mark of allegiance to the particular demons they serve. In Greece and Rome priests of Bacchus, their demon god of debauchery, left hair a bit longer on top, cut their hair on the sides of their head very short and then shaved stripes in the sides of their heads. This hairstyle was a sign of their priesthood and symbol of their allegiance to Bacchus.

3RD LESSON JOINT, ALL LADIES

Following the easy path of least resistance is what makes men and rivers crooked. People are looking for getting easy ill-gotten success. It is very rare to see rivers climbing high mountains rocks. Water goes wiggling, dogging and cutting corners where there are mountains, looking for easy flow. A river cannot go straight that is why they become crooked. Great Rivers e.g., Mississippi, Nile, Ontario, etc. are the same as some individuals, e.g. lazy people always they look for short cuts because they do not want to work or walk even when bad food, junk, is given to them, they simply eat because they do not want to be bothered with cooking, they end losing shape (obesity).

Following the easy way where there is no hardship, that is what has made people fail in life, because they want everything on silver plate. People do not want to struggle, they want the easy way of getting things. Girls have fallen in traps of evil people because they want their hair done, good clothes, good shoes, to eat good food, etc. but are not making any effort to see something which can generate income.

If you are not doing anything to help yourself a hooligan is going to come and buy a soda and chapatti and demand to have sex with you, and you cannot refuse because he has already bought you. I hope you guess what will happen, he may pregnant you or give you AIDS and that will be the end of the road for you.

My daughter Clare took a girl from here in the village to Kampala to work for her, I asked the girl to do some good crafts where I was going to be paying her at least 1,000 per piece of item, and in a day she could do about three of them, thus 3,000 per day. She could not do it, but went to the Kihura boys who sell tomatoes in Kampala, she got pregnant and she had to run back to the village.

The tomato seller one day stopped me and asked me whether I knew that girl. In the process he told me that the girl went with his pregnancy because one day he saw her with me. When she reached the village, she went and got an old man who was selling cassava flour and got married to him with her pregnancy, because of hunger.

Girls be serious, especially you who have come to know the Lord, do not desire to live easy life, it is dangerous. It cannot lead you to where you do not want to be.

When you come to the Lord count yourself of a great value because Jesus bought you with His blood. Let not boys or men use you cheaply. Be patient and wait upon the Lord, He will bring you a right person on your way when time comes.

Value Attracts Value, if you have kept yourself pure and righteous the Lord will not bring you a rogue. People are cutting heads of others because they do not want to work hard, a proverb says "If you have nothing to do the devil will get you something to do." Girls are the ones the evil people are sending to go in hospitals and steal children, new born babies and from homes disguised as house girls because they have nothing to do.

"Do not be conformed to this world, but be Renewed and Transformed in your mind, so that you may Prove what the will of God is that which is Good and Acceptable and Perfect," Romans 12:2. Do not be changed by the standards of the world, be strong and be yourself, do not see what so and so has got I have also to get it. Live within your means, that is only what you can afford.

Many people have stretched to get what so and so has got and ended in trouble. If your friend has a good dress and you borrow it, that day when you dressed in it and you go to visit or to attend a party on that day, when you take a boda-boda, that is when the dress will entangle in the wheel and it eaten up.

Be changed in your mind, so that you may prove what the will of God is for you, good and acceptable and perfect. God's will be perfect for you, except many times people want to hurry and get what they want and get the wrong ones and start blaming God that I think this one was not meant for me when things turn sour. One sees her friend is married and thinks it is so prestigious, leaves school or home so she is also going to marry. Your friend may not disclose the bad side, and you think it a bed of roses, until when you also get there, and find out the truth when it is already too late to get out.

Village marriages are so difficult unless you are prepared for it. Marriages of these days is a girl just taking herself to a boy's home, when it is not blessed and it is full of miseries because you go in disobedience. You can never be happy in it, due to poverty one cannot have a happy marriage.

There are no longer proper weddings in villages. One can take years before you hear that a son of so and so, or a daughter of so and so, is getting married unless he or she has lived in Kampala or other places. We only hear the daughter of so and so has got a child, this started long ago, since in the 1950s. This has been so because morals of people completely derailed (Ikaruga hampanga).

Let us change this marriage time, as we have come to know what God requires us. Keep yourselves completely to the Lord, He is the one who created that body you are throwing around and saying that nature cannot be stopped or controlled. It can be controlled, just try Jesus and tell Him please take care of my desires and kill them until when I will be ready to have a proper partner.

> "There are many things that catch my eye, but there are only a very few that catch my heart those I consider to pursue."
>
> AUTHOR UNKNOWN

In the world there are so many so attractive things, but you are not to take everything. Choose a few that catch your heart and pursue those. There are many boys and men you are going to meet but you are not going to run with Tom, Dick and Paul. Always take time and make your best choice and go with that, so that even when bad days come you will not regret. Job's wife left when Job got worse maybe because she had not made the commitment of well and bad times.

1 Peter 3:7 says for husbands to show wife honour as a fellow heir of the grace of life, so that your prayers will not be hindered.

Dear Ladies, the Word calls you weaker vessels, also men are weaker vessels, they are like children, they want to be pampered and cared for. Let it come to sickness, they really become like children. Even if he is a big man if you tell him come and sit on the laps, he will. I see my boys, who are now men, fit to be having homes. When he wants something he whines like a little boy. Therefore, also, be kind to them as they should also be kind to you, it is two ways. *27th - 30th April 2009*

Kangume Dancing and Worshiping God

CHAPTER 15

WHY IS SATAN FIGHTING THE CHURCH, AND NOT JESUS?

WHEN I RETURNED from the village to attend the Children's close of 2nd Term and our 1st Monthly Discussion Meeting. In attendance was Pastor Paul of Prayer Mountain, Mr. and Mrs. Bangirana, Pastor Etyeni, Mugume, Alan Mwesige and myself, Gertrude Kabatalemwa, at my home.

WHO IS FIGHTING WHO? WHY ARE THEY FIGHTING?

Spiritual Warfare Topic: The Power of Jesus Christ found in: Ephesians 1-23, 6:10,18, 5:20, and Luke 9:1. Jesus is so powerful, John 14:10 He said He is in the Father and Father is in Him. Jesus said He lives and we will also live ... I am in my Father and you are in Me and I am in you, The Lord says that "If you repent then I will restore you, if you utter worthy, not worthless, words, ... You will become my spokesman. They will come to you!! But as for you, you must not turn to them," John 14:19-21.

Therefore, thus says the Lord: "If you return, I will restore you, and you shall stand before me. If you utter what is precious, and not what is worthless, you shall be as my mouth. They shall turn to you, but you shall not turn to them. Jeremiah 15:19

Why is Satan Fighting the church, God's children and not Jesus? Sources of unrighteousness: Culture from clans and tribes. Sin from Adam and Eve. Seed is inherited from ancestors, grandparents and parents. Curses can be self caused or from other sources, gays, Rom 1:18,21,23, 25. Evil Spirits can enter a person and start using him or her like demons and fallen angels, what washes us in order to Fight effectively in the Spiritual Warfare? Fire, water, Word, Blood and Soap.

Whoever believes in Him have eternal life, John 3:15, Psalm 51, Malachi 1:7, and Isaiah 58:4. What can keep us safe in righteousness? Unity in Prayer keeps us, Maintaining righteousness and Uprooting the bad seed. True reconciliation as we Battle with ourselves, Gal. 5:6, and 2 Corinth 10:3. And reading the Word keeps us.

At around 4.00a.m the Holy Spirit woke me up with Therefore, my son, be strong in the grace that is in Christ Jesus. The things that you have heard from me in the presence of many witnesses, entrust these to faithful men who will be able to teach others also, 2 Timothy 2.

Suffer hardship with me, as good soldier of Christ Jesus. No soldier in active service entangles himself in the affairs of everyday life, so that he may please the one who enlisted him as a soldier. Also, if anyone competes as an athlete, he does not win the prize unless he competes according to the rules. The hardworking farmer ought to be the first to receive his share of the crops. Consider what I say, for the Lord will give you understanding in everything. For this reason, I endure all things for the sake of those who are chosen, so that they also may obtain the salvation which is in Christ Jesus and with it, eternal glory.

It is a trust-worthy statement: For we died with Him, we will also live with Him. If we endure, we will also reign with Him. If we deny Him, He also will deny us. If we are faithful, He is faithful for He cannot deny Himself. Remind them of these things, and solemnly charge them in the presence of God not to wrangle about words which is useless and leads to the ruin of the hearers. Be diligent to present yourself approved to God as a workman who does not need to be ashamed, accurately handling the word of truth. But avoid worldly and empty chatter, arguments, for it will lead to further ungodliness, and their talk will spread like gangrene.

The Lord knows who are His and "everyone who names the name of the Lord is to abstain from wickedness."

Now in the large house there are not only gold and silver vessels, but also vessels of wood and of earthenware, and some to honour and some to dishonour. Therefore, if anyone cleanses himself from these things, he will be a vessel for honour, sanctified, useful to the Master, prepared for every good work.

Now flee from your youthful lusts and pursue righteousness, faith, love and peace with those who call on the Lord from a pure heart. But refuse foolishness and ignorant speculations, knowing that they produce quarrels. The Lord's bond servant must not be quarrelsome, but be kind to all, able to teach patience when wronged, with gentleness correcting those who are in opposition, if perhaps God may grant them repentance leading to the knowledge of the truth, and they may come to their senses and escape from the snare of the devil having been held captive by him to do his will. *16th August 2009*

Jesus is coming again, Rev. 1:7.

CHAPTER 16

END TIME SPIRITUAL WARFARE

WE ARE LIVING in the time of the battle!

WHO IS FIGHTING WHO? ALWAYS A BATTLE ENGAGES TWO PARTIES.

So, on looking to Him who was pierced, one army is Fighting to keep looking on Him, Jesus who was pierced. For our transgressions, another army is Fighting to see that it keeps God's away from us for the reason that if we keep Jesus in view, we will win battles against satan and his lies. Therefore, there is a battle, Joel 2:1. In this battle our Commander is Jesus who is giving us instructions like Israel in the wilderness, telling us when to Camp, when to March and when to Fight.

These instructions we have to obey or else the enemy will destroy us. In the army if you are disobedient of instructions; you can easily be destroyed, Joshua. One time in 1987 there was Cadre training and instructions were to train at a certain area but they changed the location. The same army at the outpost was informed that there were rebels training, they went and shelled all the cadres and killed them because of changed instructions. Disobedience can cause you to kill each other.

The Camp, Ephesians 6:13-18, a Camp can be of a sole one person, limited to partnership of 10 members, or more than 100. In this battle the quality of a Camp determines the strength of the Army. Any Army, whether at peace or in battle, must be Waiting and Seeking the Lord. So, you have to learn when to Camp, when to March and when to Fight, (Rick Joyner).

In the Bad Camp, they destroy bridges, uproot the gardens, so no fruits are growing on bushes, torn flags, and members do not know what they are doing. There is disobedience, disorder, corruption, seeking own, self-exaltation, not focused, constant Fighting each other, wounding each other, drifting from one section to another or not steady in one place, with only 2 ranks: Generals and Privates. Generals have fake weapons, selfishness, no caring for each other, generals Fighting one another because they appointed themselves and lack, Eph. 6:13.

In any army Camp or Church like this even if you are such big numbers there will be no strength to your army of Church congregation; but weakness, more depression, wearing and tearing down. This will add no value to it, but costs more resources. One private soldier in a good Camp is more valuable than many generals in a bad Camp. This is one strong Believer, who knows to seek the Lord, even in sole Camp, and is valued more than a thousand believers sitting in a cathedral's pews.

In the Good Camp, soldiers make bridges and plant gardens, fruits are in plenty and there are high ways of righteousness. Raising flags and they know what they are doing. They are in obedience, orderly, trustworthy, and not self-seeking. Generals and other ranks work and walk together in harmony helping each other to walk, lifting each other when one falls, seeks after each other when one gets lost. Generals not thinking about themselves, friendly, determined people including men, women, children, and the old that are determined and fierce but not tense, aware of war, but with profound peace and no fear on their faces.

In this Camp generals are responsible for the condition of the soldiers, sheep, they will lay down their lives for the people of God, and prepare them for the great battle which is coming. Generals in Good Camp will not run from the Lord's circumcision, Jeremiah 9:26, Colossians 3:11. They will stand against carnality in a Camp so that the judgment does not come upon them, Num. 25. Phinehas in the Camp when he pinned down a man and woman on the ground. and the epidemic stopped there and then because the Lord was pleased with him. These generals, the Lord has called them because they love Him, they love His people and love Righteousness.

Experience of Nyamabuga Born-Again Church by Pastor Kagoro who grouped against the Youth group since April - July 2009, about accusation and counter accusation on the denied Mission. The Lord said those who want to be called by my Name but do not walk in my ways will be trodden under foot. Before the great battle my army will be Holy, even as I am Holy, 1 Peter 1:16. I will remove those who are not circumcised of heart and the leaders who do not uphold my righteousness.

Until now the Lord has called you to Camp. Most of the time has been wasted in quarrels, seeking ranks, rumours and gossiping, considering the time spent in ministry. But if you have spent all the time of prayerlessness, not seeking, etc. and only counting years in church, God is telling you that the Holy Spirit can lay hold of any common person within the church or from anywhere. Who is waiting, seeking and searching after God? He will bring them to a place of total surrender to reach God's people in communities, cities and nations.

David Wilkerson, Time Square Church, NY, gave an

example of Apostle Paul in a small house on the street from Rome to Jerusalem people came streaming looking for him. God can use the most humble anyone who is willing to be stripped and circumcised in his heart of all the pride and confidence in the flesh.

I am a Pastor, when they say lift your hands up, you say how can I do that? You are sowing disobedience. When it comes time for you also to give instructions, your subordinates also will disobey you, and you may start complaining, yet that is what you also sowed. When you do something wrong you do not want to be corrected, you say who are they to correct me?

I am a Pastor. I think you know what disobedience has done and what is happening in Kampala. Pastors have decided to go to accuse each other on TVs and Radios, now the world of the unsaved can judge the children of God. Do not judge a Book by its Cover, God can use anybody who opens his or her heart.

Azusa Street Pastor William J. Seymour prayed for hours with his head inside a wooden box, this caused Modern Day Pentecostal movement.

In reading "The Call" the Lord said He is leading His people with a clear objective and calling them to Camp with a purpose. The strength of the Army that is Marching will be determined by the Quality of the Camp (Church body of Christ). Here again, let me emphasize the Camp/Church. What is a Church? Is it a building? You can be a Camp or Church, within yourself. For me in 1987 when I was so disturbed by so many Church Doctrines a False Prophet came from London through Ghana to the Church where I was fellowshipping and I did not feel comfortable with his teaching.

I told the Lord, Please, lead me, direct me and guide me or else I am falling away. He told me; come out of those Camps and wait (Camp on your own) I will be your Pastor, your Teacher, your Director until when I tell you where to go (to March). First

He took me to Singapore, he made somebody suggest my name to go for Leadership Training. Then Bro Morris Cerrulo invited me to go the USA where He used me greatly. An Old lady who was 73 years of age, now she is 93 years, she took me to high places in USA, up to the Home of the Presidents of the USA of America for giving my testimony. Because the Lord told me When to Camp, When to March, and When to Fight. Since that time I have never been the same.

When the Lord says "Stop" and "Camp," for a season it is to teach you His Ways obey His command. You must learn when and where to Camp. At times Christian's Camp in wrong places when people will tell you where to be able to get your healing. You have to sweep the church yard, carry jerrycans of water, and use anointing oil in your hankie to place on a girl or a boy and they will follow you. In a Camp they tell you we light candles before we pray and believe in holy water. In some Camps they tell you to pay a certain amount of money before we pray for you. At times you may Camp at a wrong time, e.g. king David when the army was out Fighting for him, he went to Camp, you know what happened later with the wife of Uriah. He fornicated, murdered and stayed for almost a year without repenting until Prophet Nathan was sent to him.

You must learn when to March, e.g. Jericho walls, Saul, 1 Samuel 5:9. Old Prophet, 1 Kings 13:4-10. Moses struck the rock twice, to be killed. You have to follow Marching orders: Joshua 7:36. Great men were killed by Ai because Achan took an accursed thing, and in 1 Kings: the story the Lord said destroy everything, he disobeyed the instructions and he perished with his household. Other people March when they are told not to March, you may find you are marching to the wrong music from radio impact using songs in shrines, cults, Moslems, etc.

You must learn how to Fight and when to Fight, using correct weapons, many Christians have gone to Fight using physical, carnal weapons and were destroyed. In April - May 2009 there was a battle as a Pastor in Kampala was accused of homosexuality we heard on the radio. He went to renovate a police barracks; and later he was giving in tunes of millions to police CIDs to destroy statements and cause the accusers to denounce their statements. Some other situations cannot go without fasting and praying as the Lord told His Disciples. You have to Fight with Holy Scriptures and your life has to be pure when you go to Fight. Many times the Lord would tell Israelites to purify themselves when He was going to send them to Fight.

Brethren, know when to Camp, when to March and when to Fight. Many Christians have Camped when they were supposed to March and Marched when it was time to Fight. You will not do any one of these well unless you do them all well. So, the Lord told Rick Joyner to Camp, March and Fight at right times always. The Lord may direct you to Camp when you are thinking it is time to March because He sees things that you can never see.

The 8th February 1987 was a Sunday, I was preparing to go to Church when the Lord said "No, you are not going to church today." I started arguing with Him. I thought it was time to go to March, but He was telling me to Camp. He had seen that the Lebanese were going to execute the 4 American journalists if the American Government did not persuade the Israelites to release their 400 war prisoners accused of terrorism.

If you follow the Lord, you will always do right, think right, walk right at the right time, even though it may not seem right to you. Few of the Lord's people are equipped for battle, those who are leading now are following their own desires. The Lord is now raising up leaders who are going to train and equip His people, who are going to follow Him as the Captain of the Host, Him. You have lost many battles because you attacked the enemy when the Lord did not give you a command; or you attacked the enemy with an untrained army and you were defeated. When demons attack, I have seen this myself, everyone is shouting and commanding with no right scriptures which are the weapons the Spirit understands. At times you find demons insulting or even pointing at the sins of those who are trying to drive them out and they are kind not to jump and possess them.

Leaders have done this also because they are seeking their own glory, interest, and egos while others have God at heart and sincere motives for victory over evil for the Lord's sake. But they were not trained well, as well as their people, and did not ask the Lord for the Spirit of Wisdom.

Now it is time, do not be discouraged, the Lord is going to raise up leaders who will only March when He gives orders and Obey His command. It will win every battle and destroy the enemy. The Lord will be in the midst of us to tread His enemies under our feet. He is coming to be the Captain of the Host. So, lift up your eyes and look at that one who was pierced.

LIVING A VICTORIOUS LIFE, THE BEST OF A.W. TOZER

Everything is wrong until God sets it right. It is easy to learn the doctrine of personal revival and victorious living; it is quite another thing to take our cross and walk on to the dark and bitter hill of Calvary of self-renunciation. Here many are called but few are chosen. For every one that actually crosses over into the promised land many stand for a while, and look longingly across the river, and then turn sadly back to the comparative safety of the sandy wastes of their old lives. My experience of the Big Gate and a narrow gate in the dream. The best way to control our thoughts is to offer the mind to God in complete surrender, then the Holy Spirit will take control immediately. Train your thoughts by long periods of daily prayer. Long mental prayer talking to God inwardly as in our daily activities. 19th - 23rd May 2009

CHAPTER 17

CALL UPON THE LORD

AS I WAS RETURNING from the village, I was so tired after a week of long meetings and a long drive. As I entered the office I felt heaviness and gloom so I decided to pray; the Spirit revealed to me that "there is a black cloud" and this cloud results from people with negative wishes, words, expectations, anticipation and imaginations.

This empowers the principalities and rulers of the air to create a black cloud above that follows someone and shadows that is a coverage for the demons which walk causing people walking, in offices, homes, markets etc. a loss of the life, business, unhappiness, worry, doubt, abuse, disobedience, etc.

Out of this cloud comes repulsive slimes, vomit, urinating and defecating from demons upon the Christians who are not awake in Prayer, not fasting, nor seeking the Lord. They think that these are blessings from God and that this is anointing from the Holy Spirit. The enemy has false blessings he gives to deceive children of God and they call them God's blessings. When you are a Christian and if you go and fornicate and you get a child you come with the child and give A testimony; you go and steal money and buy a phone you come and tell the brethren that He has blessed you with a phone, it goes on with gays and homosexuals.

This cloud and shadow co-ordinate to create people's unhappy situations like terrible dreams, visions, fake revelations from principalities or rulers above and ground demons collaborate with underworld demons confusing man and causing difficult situations.

You should pray and destroy the dark cloud and its shadow which keeps following you and Call Upon the Lord to create a white cloud like that which followed the Israelites as they were coming out of Egypt. Ask the Lord to send rains of blessing, peace, joy and create positive situations where you go. 21st May 2009

CHAPTER 18

A WISE MAN

WISDOM OF THE LORD, Who can count a number of hairs on one man's head? Who can number the sand on the seashore? Who can count the raindrops? Who can number the days of eternity? Who can stop the waves of the sea with a grain of sand? Who can feed a blue whale 8 tons of krill a day? Only the Almighty.

The person with wisdom plans his days well, day to day. He does not eat all what he can eat and starve the next day. He does not spend all his days wearing out without thinking of storing riches where there are no cockroaches and rats that can destroy his treasures.

> *A wise person spends time working on earthly chores and remembers to store some good works for the day when they will not be able to put up much.*

A German motto said "What I spent was gone, what I saved I lost and what I gave I have." Thus, what I Spent lavishly on women, gambling, drinking, buying witchcraft to destroy others you can no longer see. What they saved not sharing with your friends, like land can be taken, animals die, property can either be sold or confiscated. But what you have given for a good cause to the poor, orphans, and widows those riches you have stored where there are No cockroaches.

At times you ask yourself what is wealth or riches? Benny Hinn defined riches or prosperity as: "It is a need which is met in time." You do not have many buildings, vehicles, or miles of land. But when you want to sleep in a good house it is there either you rent it or is given to you. If you need to travel at any time you can reach your destination whether you hire, you drive or use public means but you will be there the time you want to be there.

At times you feel strange among many who regard money, honour, and success as important issue of life. This was painted on the Coffin of a once wealthy man. "Sic Transit Gloria Mundi," meaning "So passes the Glory of this World." Therefore, there are so many Glories which are tearing people from God their Creator.

A wise man does not spend all his strength on things which are temporary but spares strength to use it on valuable things which will count, remember your Creator in the days of your youth. Before the sun and the light and the moon and stars grow darkened, and the clouds return after the rain, this symbolizes of old age. When the guardians of the house tremble, this symbolizes the arms in old age. And the strong men are bent, this symbolizes of the legs start bending in old age. When the grinders are idle and few, this symbolizes the molars or teeth. And those who look through the window grow dim; this lips. And the sound of the mill is low, this symbolizes a strong sound grows low in ears.

Daughters of song are suppressed, this symbolizes the trembling aged voice. And the fears of heights, this symbolizes the fear of climbing of the aged. When the almond tree blossoms, this symbolizes gray hair of the aged; and the locusts grow sluggish, this symbolizes of stiffness of movement in old age. Remember Him before the silver cord is snapped, and the golden bowel is broken, this symbolize life.

Be wise and always wait upon the Lord, store your treasures and strength to where it will be returned to you in full when your days on this earth have ended. 23rd *May* 2009

With Mother

CHAPTER 19

MY PURPOSE DRIVEN LIFE

DAY ONE, it is not all about I discovered my identity and purpose through a relationship with Jesus Christ. God was thinking of me long before I ever thought about Him. My purpose of life predates my conception. He planned it before I existed.

Day Two, I am not an accident, God prescribed every single detail of my body. He deliberately chose my race, where I will be born and where I will live, colour of my skin, hair and all my features for His purpose. He custom made me the way he wanted it and He will fulfill His purpose in me.

Day Three, Living on purpose is the path to Peace, without God, life makes no sense. Well-formed love banishes fear. Things do not change, a car is still the same, your beautiful wife is still the same but sooner or later you get bored then you want a newer one, bigger or better version. Those who follow the crowds usually get lost in it. Be Yourself. Nugget 1: "God made you an original. Following the path of least resistance is what makes men and rivers crooked." One of the hardest things about climbing the ladder of success is getting through the crowd of copies at the bottom. The key to failure is to try to please everyone. You are not created to be all things to all people, John Mason.

Until the time when you will discover your purpose that is when you will begin to live. You need Hope to cope, hope comes from having a purpose. Purpose Driven Living leads to a simpler lifestyle and saner (sane) schedule. A Plain and Simple Life is a full life and leads to Peace of Mind; because you do not hassle with worldly people, so and so has this, I have to have it too. You become selective by being selective. Creating an earthly legacy or confidence this is short sighted, but using time wisely to build an eternal legacy is long sighted and more beneficial.One day you will stand before God - who will audit your life with a Final Examination.

Dream in 2004, We were sitting in a room, each person was doing his or her hand work and waiting for the Supervisor to come and inspect our work. I saw people doing different beautiful crafts some with white laces and I was admiring. Then it turned into an Examination room. Each one was given papers to write whatever he has been doing.

When I turned to look behind many people were busy writing, some things which I could not make sense of. After writing pages I saw them tearing the pages and trying to start again, others had written for all the time which was given to them but had written only a paragraph. Another had written so much that did not make sense, he crumpled his work and threw it in the dust bin. I wondered if he was going to write enough because time was almost over.

One person next to me grabbed my paper and started copying from mine and I let him copy from mine to his. At the far end I saw the Supervisor had already arrived, he had started from the back to see the work and he was moving slowly from person to person and wagging his head. I had written pages and pages of good stuff. Immediately he was on my side and saw the person next to me how he was copying from me. I grabbed my papers from him. The Supervisor was kind of cross with me to let another person copy what I had written and he gave me a stern warning "Never! Never! give your work to be copied by someone else." I woke up from the sleep.

> *Two questions God will ask you on that Day are first, what did you do with my Son Jesus Christ? And second, what did you do with what I entrusted with you?*

Day Four, God has planted eternity in the hearts of human heart. Eccl.3:11; I was created to last forever. God designed me/you in His image, to live for eternity. Our body will end its journey on the earth ends when our heart stops beating, but it will not be the end of me. Earthly life offers many choices, you can be single, married, nun, priest, drunkard, etc. but eternity offers only two: Heaven when you say "Thy Will be done," or Hell when you say "All right then let me have it my way."

The closer you live to God, the smaller everything else appears. Worldly life and its glitters no longer attracts you die to self, people see you and wonder what you are after, you cannot run after fame, publicity, money because you are like a calm sea, (Maizi Gatekere, Nyanja Eradde). Your values change, you use your time and money more wisely, you place a higher premium or price tag, on relationships and character instead of fame or wealth or achievements or even fun. You will choose people who will help you to climb up, not those who try to bring you down in shame or those who place you on a high wall and they switch off the light and remove the ladder.

A story of 2008 Miss Uganda, when asked why she prefers boys to be her friends she said boys are genuine unlike girls who are picky. She will tell you that "you are so smart" when you are not, then she will go and dress to kill and to outsmart you when you are on an occasion. Every action good or bad of my/your life strikes some chord that will vibrate in eternity (heaven). What will eternity be like? "No mere man has ever seen, heard or even imagined what wonderful things God has made for those who love the Lord." It would be like trying to describe the Internet to a tiny book bug.

In heaven we will be reassigned Work to do with Joy, we will not lie on the clouds with halos playing harps, where one day Jesus will say "Come you who are blessed by my father, take your inheritance, the kingdom prepared for you since the creation of the World." We need to think about Eternity more, not less. Only a fool would go through life unprepared.

Think of the nine months in the womb of your mother were they not in themselves but preparation for another life. The End of your Life on earth will result in your Birth Day into Eternal Life, our life on the earth is just like a blink of an eye but the consequences of it will last forever, the deeds of this life are the destiny of the next. Be careful what you do because every time you do right or wrong a gong continues striking in heaven.

Day Five, character is both developed and revealed by test and all of life is a test. You are always being tested and God constantly watches your response to people, problems, success, conflict, illness, disappointment and even the weather! God can also intentionally draw back and we do not sense his closeness in order to bring out your true weakness or even to prepare you for more responsibility. To understand people ask them, "How do you see your life?" Responses are: It's a circus, a mine field, a roller coaster, a puzzle, a symphony, a journey, a dance, a carousel, etc. At the end of your life on earth you will be evaluated and rewarded according to how well you handled what God entrusted to you, that is everything you do say even simple daily chores have eternal implications. "If you are untrustworthy about worldly wealth, who will trust you with the true riches of heaven."

Day Six, Lord, remind me how brief my time on earth will be. Remind me that my days are numbered, and that my life is fleeing away. I am here on earth for just a little while, our days on earth are as transient as a shadow, read Psalm 119:19. You won't be here long, so do not get too attached, the Bible uses terms like: alien, pilgrim, foreigner, stranger, visitor and traveler. Friends, this world is not your home, and so do not make yourselves cozy in it. Do not indulge your ego at the expense of your soul. In God's eyes, the greatest heroes of faith are not those who achieve prosperity, success and power in this life, but those who treat this life as a temporary assignment and serve faithfully, expecting their promised reward in eternity.

> *A story of a retiring Missionary coming home to America on the same boat as the President of the United States. Cheering Crowds, a military band, a red carpet, banners and the media welcomed the president home, but the missionary slipped off the ship unnoticed. Feeling self-pity and resentment, he began complaining to God.*
> *Then God gently reminded him, "But my child, you are not home yet." Also my return from the State in 1993 at the Airport Entebbe I came back with our Traditional king, as I was walking out he was changing to traditional attire, outside dancers and big crowds were waiting for him. I slipped out but that king by 1994 died mysteriously.*

We are children of the King and His eyes are

upon us. On 10th June 2009 I had good time with the Lord as He was telling me so many of life's journeys. One young man who was one of the FDC party's strong activists was killed on 6th June 2009. The Lord said "I have given people gifts, Tom Jjurunga 28 years old had a great gift of putting ideas together assessing and analyzing situations, but he used the gift in the world which does not give security and his gift got him killed." Now if Tom had used this gift for the kingdom of God he would not have been killed like that. So, we fix our eyes not on what is seen, but of what is unseen. For what is seen Is Temporary but what is unseen is Eternal, 2 Corinthians 4:18.

Day Seven, everything comes from God alone. Everything lives by His power and for His glory, Romans 11:36. Everything He made it for His own purpose, Romans 16:4.

Every time I opened my Bible or any other book there comes a tiny insect twice smaller than little dot. It moves across the page, I leave whatever I am reading and follow it's movement and wonder what it ate, how it gives birth, how big is its brain, how it lives and how many times it doubles in an ant, then I would just give God the Glory who made the biggest creature and the smallest insect, He made everything that exists including you for His glory. Where is the glory of God? Just look around. Everything created by God reflects His glory in some way. God is powerful, He enjoys variety, loves beauty, is organized, wise and creative.

The heaven declares the glory of God. The city of God does not need the sun or the moon to shine on it, for the glory of God gives it light. God's inherent glory is what He possesses because He is God. Glory is His nature you cannot add anything to His glory, just as it is impossible to make the sun shine brighter.

In the entire universe, only two of God's creations fail to bring glory to Him: 1. Fallen angels (demons and people) and 2. Moslems, who say "There is no God but Allah." Catholics worship Mary, refusing to bring glory to God is prideful rebellion and it is the sin that caused satan's fall.

We bring glory to God by serving others without gifts. Each of us is uniquely designed by God with talents, gifts, skills and abilities manage them well so that God's generosity can flow through you, e.g. helping others, singing, counseling, etc. The way you are wired is not accidental. Living for the glory of God may require a change in your priorities, schedules, relationships and everything else, it may need to change to a difficult path instead of an easy one.

> The Bible says Anyone who holds on to Life as it is, destroys that life. But if you let it go, you will have it forever, real and eternal.

Day Eight, I was created for God's Pleasure. God wired me with five senses and emotions so that I can experience it. He created me in His image. God has emotions too, He grieves, gets jealous or angry, and feels' compassion, pity, sorrow, sympathy, happiness, gladness, and satisfaction. He loves, delights in pleasure, rejoices, enjoys and even laughs. He wants me to enjoy life but not to endure it.

Bringing pleasure to God is called Worship, worship is far more than music, a particular style of music, i.e. slow and quiet or with lifting hands, it has nothing to do with style, volume or speed of song. But whatever is Offered to God In Spirit and Truth brings God pleasure and that is worship. It is like a diamond, worship is multifaceted. Worship can be a life style, thus whatever you do to glorify God, even when one starts a gossip and you stop it and say "please, let us stop that it is annoying God, it brings pleasure to God and it is worship.

Worship is not for your benefit, Worship is not part of your life but it is Your Life. We should praise Him from sunrise to sunset wherever we are. We worship for God's benefit, to bring pleasure to our creator. The people come near to God with their mouths and honour Him with their lips, but their hearts are far from Him. Their worship of Me is made up only of rules taught by men," Isaiah 29. Hypocritical worshiping is when people just worship with their lips and not from the heart.

Day Nine, May the Lord smile on you, Numbers 6:25. Smile on me, your servant, teach me the right way to live, Psalms 119:135. Pleasing God is the first purpose of your life, so figure out what will please Christ, and then do it. Noah was a pleasure to God, Gen 6:8, he loved God above everything else even though God was grieved and regretted making man and considered wiping out the human race. God smiles when we trust Him completely.

Noah pleased God, by faith he built a ship in the middle of the dry land. He became intimate with God because he was warned about something he could not see, and acted on what he was told as a result he pleased God. God one day came to Noah and said I am disappointed in all human beings in the entire world, no one but you thinks about me!!! When I look at you, I start smiling. I am pleased with your life, so I am going to flood the world and start over with your family. I want you to build a giant ship that will save you, your family and the animals.

God smiles when we obey Him wholeheartedly and when we praise and thank Him continually and when we praise God for who He is, and we thank Him for what he has done. An amazing thing happens when we offer praise and thanksgiving to God. When we give God enjoyment, our own hearts are filled with Joy, so True, I have that experience.

Because one individual had pleased God the human race and the animal population was saved from a worldwide flood. This required great attention to logistics and details, everything had to be done just as God prescribed it. We please God by what we do and not by what we believe or reason in our heads.

Day Ten, Heart of Worship, give yourself to God and your whole being to be used for righteous purposes, Romans 6:13. Surrender and submission implies losing a Fight or battle, no one wants to be a loser! It evokes a shameful, unpleasant image of admitting defeat in battle, forfeiting a game or yielding to a stronger opponent like boxers or wrestlers. The word is almost always used in a negative context. Captured criminals surrender to authorities, e.g. Escobar a Mexican a notorious drug dealer and Carlos the Jackal arrested in Sudan when he was given so much to come and assassinate M7, but M7 because prayers covering him went and said that the man was highly guarded he was living in glass walls which he could not break through.

The popular teaching these days is: winning, overcoming, conquer, success, etc. instead of yielding, submitting, obeying and surrendering. In today's competitive culture we hear "Never give up" and "Never give in."

Surrendering to God is the heart of worship, and the natural response to God's amazing love and mercy. We give ourselves to Him not out of fear or duty, but of love, because "He first loved us." True worship brings God pleasure when you give yourself completely to God. Personal surrender to God can be referred to: Consecration, Yielding to the Spirit, making Jesus your Lord, Taking Up your Cross, Dying to Self, God wants your life, all of it.

The three barriers that block total surrender to God are Fear, Pride, and Confusion, you cannot trust God until you know Him better. **Fear** keeps us from surrendering, Love casts out all fear, when fear knocks at the door of your heart, let faith open the door. Fear may say you will die at the end of this year. Let Faith say "No" I shall not die but will live to tell the goodness of the Lord, Psalm 118:17.

HOW DO YOU KNOW THAT GOD LOVES YOU?

The evidence is clear:

- God says He loves you!!!
- You are never out of His sight,
- He cares for every detail of your life,
- He gave your capacity to enjoy all kinds of pleasures,
- He has good plans for your life,
- He forgives you for all your iniquities,
- He is patient with you,
- God loves you infinitely more than you can imagine, John 3:16.

To prove all that, look at Him with His arms outstretched on the cross saying "I Love You This Much," He said He would rather die than live without you.

God is not a cruel slave driver or a bully who uses cruel brute force to coerce us into submission, No!!! He woos us to Himself in order to offer ourselves freely to Him. God is a Lover and a Liberator, when we surrender to Him it brings freedom, not bondage, He is not a tyrant but a Saviour, not a boss but a Brother, not a dictator but a Friend.

Admitting our Limitations, the second barrier to surrender is our **Pride**, the desire to have complete control (BoM example is head of a family with chicken or meat) this is the cause of so much stress in our lives. Some people want to be like God, what we cannot be and will not be, we are human beings and that's it. When we try to be God, we end up being more like satan who desired the same thing who thought to be like the Most High and set his throne above.

A.W. Tozer said the reasons why many are still troubled, still seeking, still making little forward progress is because they haven't yet come to the end of themselves." We are still trying to give orders and interfering with God's work within us." We are humans with limitations like emotions or analyzing life with human head knowledge; when we are faced with our own limitations we react with irritation, anger and resentment.

We want to be taller like Johnson, strong like Tyson, talented like Eddie Murphy, beautiful like Madonna and wealthier than Bill Gates. When all this does not happen we become upset because we want to have it all. And then we notice others characteristics we do not have we respond with envy, jealousy and self-pity thinking that because of my family back ground then we blame our father if he had taken me further.

We judge that they cheated on an exam or finger point at them is the one who caused me suffering, and so on.

What it means to surrender, surrendering to God is not a passive resignation, fatalism or an excuse for laziness. It is not accepting the status quo known as the existing state of affairs. It may mean the exact opposite, sacrificing your life and/or suffering in order to change what needs to be changed. God often calls surrendered people to do battle on His behalf, people like Pastor Sempa and Kyazze vs Kayanja.

SURRENDERING IS NOT FOR COWARDS OR DOORMATS.

God would not waste the mind He gave you! God does not want robots to serve Him, He wants to use your unique personality. C.S. Lewis observed that "It is when I turned to Christ, when I gave up myself to His personality, that I first began to have a real personality of my own." You will know you are surrendered when you do not react to criticism and rush to defend yourself. Surrendered hearts show up best in relationships.

You do not edge others out, you do not demand your rights, and you aren't self-serving when you are surrendered; this means your money too, though it is very difficult for many people with their money. "You cannot serve both God and money." Genuine surrender says: "Father, if this problem, pain, sickness or circumstance of Robert and Peter is needed to fulfill your purpose and glory in my life or in another's, please do not take it away." This level of maturity does not come easy. Surrender is hard wok. In our case, it is intense warfare against our self-centered nature.

The Blessings of Surrender, benefits of surrender when you fully surrender your life to God are many. You Experience Peace. You Stop quarreling with God. You Agree with God and things go well for you. You Experience Freedom that never quits. You Experience God's Power in your life. You Defeat stubborn temptations and overwhelming problems.

In Joshua a story tells of a Surrender that led to a stunning victory at Jericho, this is a paradox and is self-contradictory, say I am a thief. Surrendered people are the ones God uses. God chose Moses, Joseph, Esther, Mary, etc. Everybody eventually surrenders to something or someone. If not to God you will surrender to the opinion or expectation of others, to money, resentment, fear or to your own pride, lusts and/or ego.

You were designed to worship God, and if you fail to worship Him, you will create other things called idols to give your life to. E. Stanley Jones said "if you do not surrender to Christ, you will surrender to Chaos," Victory Through Surrender. Put Jesus Christ in the driver's seat of your life and take your hands off the steering wheel. Do not be afraid, nothing under His control can ever be out of control.

Mastered by Christ, you can handle anything. This is a warning: when you decide to live a totally surrendered life, that decision will be tested. Sometimes it will mean doing inconvenient, unpopular, costly or seemingly impossible tasks. It will often mean doing the opposite of what you feel like doing. You may find yourself doing something you have never dreamt about, i.e.

after leaving the civil Servant Job, I never had a dream of what I am doing, starting and managing schools.

A question was forwarded to Bill Bright, the founder of Campus Crusade for Christ, asking "Why did God use and bless you your life so much?" He said When was a young man, I made a contract with God. I literally wrote it out and signed my name at the bottom, it said "From this day forward, I am a slave of Jesus Christ."

Day Eleven, God wants to be our friend. Your relationship to God has many different aspects: God is your Creator, Maker, Lord, Master, Judge, Redeemer, Father, Saviour and so on, but the most shocking truth is this: Almighty God yearns to be your friend.

Friendship with God is possible only because of the grace of God and the sacrifice of Jesus. It is important to establish the habit of daily devotional time with God. Becoming a best friend of God through constant conversation. You will never grow a close relationship with God by just attending church once a week or even by having a daily quiet time. Friendship with God is built by sharing all your life experiences with Him. He wants to be included in every activity, every conversation, every problem, and even every thought. You can carry on a continuous, open-ended conversation with Him throughout your day, talking with Him about whatever you are doing or thinking at that moment, by Praying without ceasing.

Everything you do can be "spending time with God, if he is invited to be a part of it and you stay awake of His presence, Practicing the Presence of God. Begin doing for God what you normally do for yourself like eating, bathing, working, relaxing or taking out trash even sleeping for God. Pray shorter conversational prayers continually through the day rather than trying to pray long session of complex prayers.

To maintain focus and counteract wandering thoughts do not

use multitude of words in prayer. Choose brief sentences or simple phrases that can be repeated to Jesus in one breath: You are with me, I receive Your grace, I am depending on You, I want to know You, I belong to You, Help me to trust You, For me to live is Christ, You will never forsake nor leave me, You are my God." Practicing the Presence of God is a Skill and Habit you can develop. Prayer lets you speak to God; and Meditation lets God speak to you! Both are essential to becoming a friend of God.

Day Twelve, draw close to God, and God will draw close to you, James 4.8. You are close to God as you choose to be. You must work at developing your relationship with God. It won't happen by accident. It takes desire, time and energy. Choose to be honest with God. The first building block of a deeper friendship with God is complete honesty about you faults and your feelings. God doesn't expect you to be perfect, but He does insist on complete honesty.

None of God's friends in the Bible were perfect. To be God's friend, you must be honest with God, sharing your true feelings, not what you think you ought to feel or say. Tell God exactly how you feel. We harbor resentment towards God over our appearance, background, unanswered prayers, past hurts and other things we would change if we were with God. People always blame God for hurts caused by others.

This creates what William Bachus wrote about in a book called Your Hidden Rift With God.

"Bitterness is the greatest barrier to friendship with God."

WILLIAM BACHUS

It is encouraging to know that all of God's closest friends Abraham, Moses, David, Elijah and Job had bouts with doubt, but instead of masking their misgivings with pious clichés, they candidly voice them openly and publicly. Expressing doubts is sometimes the first step towards the next level of intimacy with God.

We are friends with God but we are not equals. He is our loving leader and we follow Him. True friendship is not passive, it acts. Jesus asks us to Love others, help the needy, share our resources, keep our lives clean, offer forgiveness and bring others to Him. Love motivates us to obey Jesus immediately.

Where was Jesus for thirty years that gave God so much pleasure? The Bible says it was "Lived obediently." The more you become God's friend, the more you will care about the things He cares about, grieve over the things He grieves over, and rejoice over the things that bring pleasure to Him. To be a friend of God, you must care about all the people around you that God cares about. Friends of God tell their friends about God.

Day Thirteen, Love the Lord your God with all your heart and with all your mind and with all your strength, Mark 12:30. God wants all of you!!! A Samaritan woman, Jesus told her, it does not matter whether you worship in Jerusalem, the time is coming when those who worship Him will not mind the time, place and style for worship, but only that they who worship Him in Spirit and Truth, John 4:24. So, let us be grateful and worship Him in a way that will please Him.

CHAPTER 20

CHARACTERISTICS OF WORSHIP THAT PLEASE GOD

ACCURATE WORSHIP BASED on the Word not our opinion about God.

Do you say I like to think of God as... , like Indians with elephants, rivers and tree worshipping, they pain create idols of their own desired gods, or images of god and worship it, this is idolatry.

If you do not worship the true God, you will worship a fake idol.

Authentic worship in the spirit is not referring the Holy Spirit but your Spirit made in God's image. He designed it to communicate with Him only they respond to each other. When we worship, He sees the attitude of our hearts. We worship Him with deep feelings and emotions which are genuine not fake. God hates hypocrisy, showmanship, pretense, phoniness, but only approves honest real love.

Today people are equating being emotionally moved by

music as if moved by the spirit, these are two different things. Real worship happens when your spirit responds to God and not to musical tones. Some sentimental, introspective songs take the spot light off God and focus on our feelings.

The best style of worship is the one which authentically represents your love for God based on the background and personality God gave you, jolly, crying, singing own hearty songs, i.e. one sister who used to sing only in a flat voice started singing worship to God, her friend rebuked her because she did not have a good voice to sing, but she replied "I am not singing for you, I am singing for the Lord."

God intentionally made us differently but everyone is expected to love in the same way. Gary Thomas discovered ways to enjoy intimacy with God, one can go to the mountain to Seek Him, Study the Word, Sing, Read, Dance, Creative Art, Serving Others, Solitude, Fellowship, etc.

Nine ways people draw near to God:

1. Naturalist: are inspired to love God out of doors, natural settings, falls, animals, birds, flowers, (Mweya, Machison).
2. Sensate: gifted physical feelings of love for God by their senses, appreciation of beautiful breathtaking scenery, of a worship service that involves sight, taste, smell and touch.
3. Traditionalist: Draw closer to God through rituals, liturgies, symbols and public service like evangelists and crusaders.
4. Aesthetic: Drawing closer to God with your own plan as in through solitude, simplicity, or separation for the reason of worshipping the beauty of God.
5. Activist: Draw close to God through confrontation of

evil and battling injustice, working to make the world a better place, (Pastors Sempa and Kyazze).
6. Care Giver: Love God by loving others and meeting their needs (Clare) cannot feel good until she gives.
7. Enthusiastic: Love God through passionate celebration, like dancing, music shows.
8. Contemplative: Love God through adoration, lifting hands, bowing, kneeling feels taken up consumed with the love of God.
9. Intellectual: Love God by studying the Word and understanding with their mind, meditating and reasoning.

These are the kind of people the Father is looking for those who are simple and honest with themselves before Him through their worship.

Thoughtful worship, because God is not pleased with thoughtless singing of hymns, repeated clichés or careless exclamations of "Praise the Lord!" If worship is mindless it is meaningless, you must engage your mind, using fresh words e.g. I admire you Lord, I respect you, I value you, I revere you, I honor you and I appreciate you.

In worship we are to "offer our bodies as living sacrifices." Now, we usually associate the concept of "sacrifice" with something, ding, but God wants you to be a living sacrifice. He wants you to live for Him! Except the problem with a living sacrifice is that it can crawl off the altar, and we often do that. We sing, "Jesus we are here for you" when we are darting on some streets doing window shopping or quarreling with someone or we are here on Sunday then on Monday we are doing our own things. Worshiping, as if you were forced, is an oxymoron, your worshipping is meaningless and the combination of worshipping and forced these are two contradictory words: cruel kindness.

And anytime worship, when you praise God even when you do not feel like it, when you get out of bed to worship when you are tired, or when you help others when you are worn out, you are offering a sacrifice of worship to God. That's what pleases God. You can Feel in your heart and your whole being that worship.

CHAPTER 21

THE BEST WAY TO SPELL LOVE IS "T I M E,"

DAY FOURTEEN, the Lord has hidden Himself from His people but I trust Him and place my hope in Him, Isaiah 8:17. God is real no matter how you feel. The deepest level of worship is praising God in spite of pain, thanking God during a trial, trusting Him when tempted, surrendering while suffering, and loving Him when He seems distant. Friendships are often tested by separation and silence; you are divided by physical distance or you are unable to talk. In your friendship with God, you won't always feel close to Him.

"Any relationship involves times of closeness and times of distance, and a relationship with God times of faith and times of unbelief. No matter how intimate, the pendulum will swing from one side to the other,"

PHILIP YANCEY

To mature your friendship, God will test it with periods of seeming separation and times when it feels as if he has abandoned or forgotten you. God feels a million miles away.

St. John of the Cross referred to it as days of spiritual dryness, doubt and estrangement from God as "the dark night of the soul." Henry Nouwen called it "the ministry of absence." A.W. Tozer recalled it "the ministry of the night," while others refer to it as "the winter of the heart."

In Psalms David asks Lord why are you standing aloof and far away? Why do you hide when I need you the most? Why have you forsaken me? Why do you remain so distant? Why do you ignore my cries for help? Why have you abandoned me? The Lord says I will never leave you nor forsake you, Hebrew 13.

When you are a baby Christian God gives you a lot of confirming emotions and often answers the most immature, self-centered prayers so you will know He exists. But as you grow in faith, He will wean you off these dependencies.

Always tell God how you feel, pour your heart to God. Unload every emotion that you are feeling. Job prayed I can't be quiet, I am angry and bitter, I have to speak! O, for the days when I was in my prime, when God's intimate friendship blessed my house. God can handle your doubt, anger, fear, grief confusion and questions. Never doubt in the dark what God told you in the light.

Day Fifteen, You were formed for God's family. You became part of the human family by your first birth, but you become a member of God's family by your second birth by being Born Again in the Spirit. Your Spiritual family is more important than your physical family because your spiritual family will last forever.

Day Sixteen, life is all about Love. Best use of life is Love. Love will last forever. On the bedside of people in their final moments, when they stand on the edge of eternity, a dying man cannot ask for his degree, diplomas, medals, objects like cars and watches to give a last look or touch except you will find him surrounded by the people he loves. In heaven God will not say "Tell me about your career, air conditioner, soccer ball game, social clubs," instead He will review how you treated others, particularly those in need.

> **Prayer**, God, please, I want to make sure that I spend time loving you and loving other people. Amen.

That is what life is all about and I do not want to waste time this day. Why should God give you another day if you are going to waste it? When you give someone your time you are giving them a portion of your life that you will never get back. Time lost cannot be traced back.

THE BEST WAY TO SPELL LOVE IS "T I M E," YOU SPEND WITH THE ONE YOU LOVE.

One time a husband who does not spend time with his family but provides all the necessities said I provide all the needs for my family what else do they want? Sir, your family want your eye contact, ears to hear your voice, words from your own mouth they want to hear your voice, spend time and presence. Nothing can take the place of that, focus attention on family. If you value a person you give him your most precious asset which is time. Best expression of love is Time.

Day Seventeen, God's family is the Church of the Living God, 1 Timothy 3:15. The church is a body of Believers not a building, an Organism not an Organization. Organizations of the body have to be connected together in order to form a complete body to fulfill the purpose You are a body of Christ. The Church Body is so significant that Jesus died on the cross for it, Christ loved the church and gave His life for it. The Church is the Bride of Christ and The Body of Christ.

CHAPTER 22

WHERE DO I DRAW MY STRENGTH?

SPIRITUALLY:

- Peace of the Lord
- Prayer
- Reading the Word, keeping and treasuring in it
- Internal Intercession
- Forgiveness
- Intimate fellowship with the Lord
- Waiting on the Lord
- Building capacity by reading books of great men of God
- Hanging on, in thin and small
- Total faith in Him who called me to salvation
- Forsaking whatever, whoever does not edify me in the spirit
- Contentment in the Lord
- Internal praise and worshiping the Lord 24 hours
- Always waiting expectantly for the Return of the Lord

- Think of the goodness of the Lord all the time
- Meditating on His goodness of the Lord and His Word

PHYSICALLY:

- Knowing who my healer is
- Drawing out my inner beauty to dominate the outer beauty
- By being original remain in the Lord's image
- Keeping my body pure without engaging it in world corruption....
- Holding myself as a Child of King
- Keeping my body inside, outside clean
- Eating right, drinking right, sleeping right
- Giving my body enough rest
- Not engaging in loose talks which toxics the body
- Be in the right place, with right people, right message and in the unity of spirit
- By avoiding worries/disappointments
- By being cheerful all the time
- Avoiding people who can contaminate me with their sweet nothing talk

MATERIALLY:

- Give whatever belongs to the Lord
- Live by helping others and the needy to feel the love of God
- Feel no worldly attachments to stand on my way
- Work Hard for my achievement 27th *June 2009*

CHAPTER 23
INNER PEACE

INNER PEACE, the previous night I had an intensive prayer encounter with the Lord, early in the morning I got this message from the Lord, John 14:27.

"Obuteeka Mumutima"
"Peace at Heart"
"Okuhumura Mumutima"

"Peace at Heart" is the most best treasure one can get in the whole world, as most people are doing whatever they are doing to get Peace at Heart. One is working hard to get money and be well, the end results of this is having Peace at Heart. Others think that if they build beautiful homes, get new cars every six months or marry a beautiful wife and have beautiful children it will give them Peace at Heart.

Peace at Heart is only from God, not any other source. When you have Peace at Heart you have everything in the world, nothing will harass you or distract your attention, e.g. Peter and

Robert stories. The Lord said: "Peace I leave you with; my peace I give to you; not as the World gives I do give to you, John 14:27.

The Peace from the Lord gives contentment and fills the vacuum, God created man and put eternity in him, Eccl. 3:11, there is nothing that can fill him up.

Rick Joyner in his book "The Call" the Lord told him that 'if you gather all the treasures of the whole world it cannot buy one's soul even for a second. So, there is a great vacuum in man which cannot be filled except by the creator Himself. Even if one has all that the World has to offer, without the Prince of Peace you cannot have the peace, it is all vanity of vanities, you will continue craving for more. When the Peace of the Lord comes it fills the vacuum which hangs around every human being.

One may say if I get this or that I will be at rest, the vacuum has caused politicians to hang on power, e.g. Robert Mugabe of Zimbabwe at 80+ was still seeking more years to rule the impoverished country. Rich men accumulate more wealth, the richest man on the earth Aga Khan was always building empires. Polygamous men will marry more women-conman Victor Clavizzao wedded the 5th wife without divorcing the other four; New Vision newspaper of 30th June 2009 says he was sentenced to 40 years after murdering the boy friend of his new wife.

Celebrities seek more attention, MJ who had accumulated so much wealth was ill, AEG Live was organizing MJ 50 London Concerts, when he died by an overdose when he was put to sleep for four days waiting for a demon to come and give him a new hit to beat a rival pop musician Prince, then he died of an overdose, New Visions newspaper stories of 30th June 2009. There is no peace for academicians; they struggle to acquire one award after another.

You may have so much of everything in the world, without the Prince of Peace residing in your heart, you have only Battles and Confusion.

In February 1997 I waited upon the Lord in Prayer and Fasting for the visit of the USA's President Clinton as his helicopter passed by our house in Kololo at 2.00pm I heard the Lord saying I have gave you 2000% of Wisdom.

Wisdom without Internal Peace is dangerous, God gave king Solomon wisdom, riches and honor, 1 Kings 3:12b-13. King Solomon's power, wealth and wisdom. 1 Kings 4:20-22, king Solomon was so powerful his rule was from Philistines to the border of Egypt. He was wealthy to the extent that a meal a day was ten fat oxen, 20 pasture oxen, and hundred sheep, besides deer, gazelles, roe bucks and fattened chickens. Solomon turned from God, 1 Kings 11:1-4 he had seven hundred wives and princesses and three hundred concubines that turned his heart from the Lord especially in his old age. Now the Lord was angry with Solomon because his heart was turned away from the Lord. In 1 Kings 11:9-12, the Lord tore his kingdom away from him and his family and gave it to someone else.

The internal peace brings contentment, fulfillment, serenity, long life and cools anger. If great wisdom, wealth, power, honor climbs to the peak and you find you are overwhelmed, ask yourself by the way what is all this whirlwind about? When you ask yourself about that situation the storm within you will subside and the Peace of the Lord will take over the tempest of pride, you will feel calmness on the Sea of Galilee.

This is me! At times I would wake up feeling good about all of me, put on my best as if I am going to meet a dignitary from somewhere, I do not know, get to the place of work.

Then the whirlwind starts mounting: I hear my flesh telling me "Sincerely, the way you look and dress you need to at least go somewhere someone will notice you and admire you, do not even drive just walk along the streets until you are noticed." There and then "Be Noticed spirit" starts climbing to the peak and I am overwhelmed and I say "by the way, what is all this whirlwind for?"

The Spirit of Peace within me commands my flesh "sit down! Go nowhere!" Or if I am are already out, He says; "go back to the office" and that's it.

There are various whirlwinds which drive people out of their skin when they find themselves either crushed or dead; whirlwinds like anger, power, wisdom, fame, wealth, lust, jealousy, hatred, ambition, beauty, violence, greed of food or drunkenness. When people get to the climax of one of these without the inner Peace and contentment, they get drunk, and do not know how to control their flesh, it starts to dictate or drive them, eventually they find themselves crushed or dead.

At times one can be driven by a couple or more whirlwinds, e.g. Idi Amin who was possessed by power, he claimed to be a life President, fame he said he was the conqueror of the British empire, hatred, he hated all whites especially the Israelites and used to call them Zionist Imperialists, lust, had so many women one time we attended a repeated wedding, violence, he ordered many people to be killed whom he suspected could oust him, jealousy he killed boyfriends of girls he wanted to befriend or befriended because of jealousy.

In the 1980s there used to be a girl who thought she was so beautiful, she got drunk with it, so she would ask her friends "How can one manage to look so ugly?" She had no job so every morning she would dress up to kill and go to loiter in the whole city showing off her beauty. She got so drunk with it and one day a high placed official in the government fell in love with her and when the wife heard it, she hired street boys who threw acid on the beauty's face and flew to the city alleys. That was the end of her beauty, she was taken to London for plastic surgery and she died in agony after one year.

Nebuchadnezzar got drunk with power and fame and

boasted of his empire but God was so kind to him, only made him eat grass like an animal for 7 years until he recognized the supremacy of God and repented, Daniel 4:29-34.

Queen Vashti got drunk with beauty and fame she was powerful in the whole empire she lost her throne as a queen. When her husband king Ahasuerus of Persia and Media called her to come and show her beauty to the invited dignitaries the whirlwind mounted and made her forget the one who throned her a queen could be the same one who would dethrone her and she refused to come and lost her crown and palace.

Herod Agrippa, grandson of Herod the Great, king of Judea and Samaria persecuted the early Church, driven by the whirlwinds of violence, fame and power. He killed James the brother of John, cousin of our Lord, and went on ahead to imprison Peter who was later released by an angel from Prison, Acts 12:1-21.

On an appointed day Herod having put on his royal apparel took his seat on the rostrum and began delivering an address to them. The people kept crying out "The voice of God and not of a man," immediately an angel of the Lord struck him, and immediately he was eaten by worms while he was alive and so he died.

Inner Peace, the inner peace within you brings calmness, trust, obedience, love, humility and patience. Queen Esther had all those qualities and she won the throne as a Queen of Persia and Media instead of Vashti. When the 12 months after her beautification in the Harem she had to present herself to the king and she was given opportunity to take with her whatever she wanted to the palace. She did not take anything like other girls, except what Hegai, the king's eunuch advised. She trusted Hegai, who knew the king better. We should entirely Trust the Holy Spirit who knows what the father wants, Esther 2:8-10.

The Internal Peace of the Lord causes Trust, Esther found favour in the eyes of all who saw her because of the inner peace. Internal Peace enabled Esther not to hurry and make a petition when the king asked her at a banquet to ask whatever she wanted, that even if it was half of his kingdom. Peace spoke to her that; one day more will not make the meat rot.

The Lord was still working out ways and means to pin down Haman. That night when the Lord prompted the king to ask for the king's Chronicles, finding out the noble Act of Mordecai the Jew, which set the events which led Haman the Agagite to hang on the gallows which he had built for Mordecai. If Queen Esther had hurried to petition this would have tied God's hands.

Now when Daniel knew that the document was signed, he entered his house he had windows open towards Jerusalem and he continued kneeling on his knees three times a day praying and giving thanks before God, Daniel 6:10. Because of the Inner Peace and Trust in God whom he believed even then these men came by agreement and found Daniel as he continued with his petition and supplication before his God. Daniel 6:16. was cast into the lions' den.

Due to Inner Peace and Trust he had in the Lord, the king had also noticed it, so after casting him in the lions' den the king went off to his palace and started fasting and had no sleep at all. Early in the wee hours he went to the lions' den and cried in a troubled voice "Daniel, servant of the living God, has your God whom you constantly serve been able to deliver you from the lions?

Consider that, the king knew the Inner Peace and Trust Daniel had for his Lord!!! God works with us when we Wait upon Him and Trust him. With the Inner Peace when we wait patiently upon Him, He rewards us.

When I was faced with the dilemma of my son Peter who was kidnapped after the war of Amin at 2 years of age and taken to Ghana. After 22 years waiting patiently for the Lord to answer the very day I got the news of his whereabouts I was traveling from upcountry to see the Village Project and as the bus I was traveling in passed one of the Trading Centers, the Lord placed a sign post which was painted in blue and white spelling for me Patience Pays, in my spirit I heard Peter is Back.

I went back later to look for that sign post but I never saw it there up to know that was a message for me. Out of our Inner Peace we get patience, kindness, faithfulness, joy, gentleness and goodness, Galatians 5:22. If we are endowed with all these fruits, the Lord will bring and it come to pass, what man thinks is impossible for him. 27th June 2009

Boys learn to make mats

Baskets the young girls made

CHAPTER 24

KYABAROKOLE CHURCH CONFERENCE

Message for the Kyabarokole Church Conference parts are repeated earlier in this book.

THEME: My people are destroyed for lack of knowledge. Because you have rejected knowledge, I also will reject you from being My priest. Hosea 4:6

WHAT DOES THE WORD TO DESTROY MEAN? DESTROY IS TO kill, ruin, demolish or to put to end. The Lord was saying His people are being killed, ruined put to an end because of lack of knowledge. What is Knowledge? Knowledge is 1. The fact or experiences known by a person or group of people, 2. The state of knowing, 3. Specific information about a subject, and 4. to my knowledge as I understand. Knowledgeable means intelligent or well-informed.

Why are God's people destroyed? The Lord was saying and is still saying; that His people are being, killed, ruined, extinguished because of: 1. lack of facts or experience - known by a person or group of people, 2. lack of knowing the truth, 3. lack of being given specific information about a subject matter, 4. lack of knowledge as they understand.

Lack of facts or experience the People of God are destroyed due to lack of all facts pertaining to salvation, the moment they announce that they are saved they think that is the end of it. They do not get to know more about the walk of a Christian, on that level they do not seek more Knowledge. I hear that even in marriage, after a girl gets married, days later a boy's relatives take her a side to advise her on the culture of the family: Your father in law you do not call him Kato we call him Kazira, we do not call water here we call it Amatungi because that was the name of the great grandfather and so on.

New Christians after getting saved they do not sit with experienced old members to help them in the studying of the Word of God. They are not told the pillars of salvation, The Word, Prayer and Fellowship. At this level many new converts get under cooked (Kukona) and once they are under cooked, to correct them is very difficult.

One comes lying and continues lying in the church, one gets saved when they are a thief and continue stealing in the church and when you try to correct them they says this church is harassing me, I will leave this church and go to the neighboring church, or I will go back where I came from, as if where he is going God there allows him to do whatever he wants to do; eventually he starts roaming and ends up by dying in the spirit and then in the body.

Lack of knowing the whole truth and walking in total victory many People are Saved and they stop there, they need to be Born-again. They are so many people walking saved but still living in defeated life, because they are still telling lies, fornicating, stealing, hating, etc. Once you accept Jesus Christ it is not to turn 99% or 99.9%, but to turn 100% and forsake everything. Therefore, if anyone is in Christ, he is a new creature, the old things passed away behold, new things have come a new, 2 Corinthians 5:17.

There is one body and one spirit, just as also you were called in one hope of your calling; one Lord, one faith, one Baptism, one God and Father of all who is over all and through all and in all, Ephesians 4:4-6.

When you are a New Creature, a bell rings, a warning bell, whenever you have sinned, are about to sin, or are sinning the sun can never go down without you knowing that you have sinned. There are two ways of communication between man and his Creator, 1. your Talking and Listening to the Father, and 2. the Father Talking and Listening to His child.

There is Great Hunger when you get saved, you need to start in a high gear in studying His Word, in prayer, and in seeking his face. By the time the heat comes down you will be miles away from the devil and his demons, run a marathon, put a big gap for him to catch up with you.

Dream, I was in a maze and a certain old man whom I knew was following me. I walked in the maze and put a distance between me and him, but every time I was looking behind, he was trotting following at a distance, until he could no longer see me. I took a corner and changed the strategy. I found an Old Lady Pastor and she cuddled me like a baby and covered me with wrapper. Being in the spirit the old man came later and went looking for a weapon to come and finish me up, while he was gone the Lord asked me that "in such a situation what do you do?" I said "Lord, I do not want to answer in haste, let me get time and think and give the correct answer."

In a total surrendered Life people have experience hearing from God, because God talks and instructs them, and they talk to God. People who do not make a total commitment do not get benefits of getting close relationship with the Lord. Some people wonders or denies that God talks to His people, they doubt when they learn of those who have close relationship with the Lord and that He talks to them, they are pretending or day dreaming.

Some Chicago pastors from a Baptist Church who do not believe that God still talks to His people come to Uganda every year, when they listen to my testimonies of how God has been talking or instructing me, they Say Gertrude has many stories, they call them stories yet these are life giving stories. One time the Lord showed me a child who had taken poison and was going to die and the Lord woke me up at 3.00am to pray for him there and then to come back to life, then instructed me to go to pray for him, but I did not know the home where the boy was, but the Lord the next day brought somebody who knew the parents of the boy and their home. It took three days talking back and forth and God giving me instructions.

Lack of being given specific information people perish. There are many people who come to know the Lord but they have never experienced Joy, they get Joy only moments when they are at the church, the moment they leave the church premises the spirit of fear of unseen dangers start mounting, night battles with demons. When fear knocks the door let Faith open. The devil will tell you I am going to kill you this morning! Tell Him No you cannot kill me, I will live to tell the goodness of the Lord, Psalm 118:17. Fear can make you run when nobody is chasing you. Until you have completely surrendered 100%, that is when you get empowered to Fight, command and have full authority of the devil then you will experience full Joy. You need to know specific factors and truths which will lead you to victory and enjoy your walk with the Lord. If you walk in darkness and you are not aware of these facts you will die because of lack of knowledge known as ignorance.

What is a covenant (Endagaano)? It is something to say, involve, commit which is irrevocable it binds two people together drag them along. Covenants can be inherited from parents, grandparents or ancestor. You can enter into a covenant by a decision of your own for safety reasons, you may join secret society for protection like Masons to gain access to wealth, etc. or for fun. People covenanting by drinking each one's blood (Kwita omukago). Out of a covenant come a byproducts called curses, bondages and yokes.

Bondages, yokes, prison, a bondage is like a prison, many people are born in Bonded or Yoked families. These yokes or prison walls need to be broken when you have totally surrendered to the Lord. You cannot break the covenanted yokes, your great grand, of great, great grandpa made with the devil. And with acceptance alone, you cannot break the yoke. Only Jesus can break the yoke. Gen. 27:40. There are so many ways of being yoked.

Self-made yokes, Covenants, contracts, and agreements made by getting involved in witchcraft, cannibalism, idolatry, etc. by making promises without thinking first, i.e. a girl or a boy making a promise, "if you will leave me, I will kill myself." The demons of suicide are always listening. The day comes the girl or boy leaves, a suicide spirit comes and says kill yourself now. A lady called Mary cut her throat when a man she was in love with left her, though she was having other men's kids.

Marriage yokes, men marrying women who have been hooked from pagan families, like idolatry (Mbandwa, bigunguza, ndyoka, nyabiingi, ritual observed twins, cannibalism, bondages). When you marry a woman who is hooked to those satanic hooks, you also become a party to that setup. When she wants to offer sacrifice to her idols you are part of it because you will have to get meat. Or if the husband asks the wife to prepare a meal for the idols you cannot say no, so you both become a part of the idol worshipers, 1 Corinthians 10:25-32.

Sexual yokes, men or women getting involved in sex with

women; men, boys or girls who are having satanic involvement. The Lord warns that His people, Believers, should not be yoked with nonbelievers. When you are only saved and you are not born again it is easy to be lured in sexual immorality with unbelievers. The Word says: Do not you not know that your bodies are members of Christ? Shall I then take away the members of Christ and make them members of a prostitute? Or do you know that the one who joins himself to a prostitute is one body with her?

The two shall be one body, but the one who joins himself to the Lord is one spirit with him. Flee immorality. Do not you know that your body is the temple of the Holy Spirit who is in you. For you have been bought with a price; therefore glorify God in your body. 1 Corinthians 6:15-20. Do not be yoked with nonbelievers. Some men or women are agents of satan once you join together your body with them it gives an open door for the devil's agents to enter you through sex door. Some unbelievers use witchcraft to hook partners so that they do not leave them.

Incest yokes, when blood brothers and sisters join in sex together, they form covenants. If a woman has ever been involved in this type of incest, will end in broken home, children will not be fruitful. E.g. I know one family where man married his daughter, they produced beautiful 9 children girls and boys. One very beautiful girl in my family was going to marry the king but the devil came and removed her private parts mysteriously in the morning there was only a hollow and she died later.

Friend's yokes, walking with friends who may lead you to traps like smoking, marijuana, Mairungi, alcohol, seeing movies of sex, violence, and witchcraft.

Ancestral yokes, bondages of ancestral yokes of father, mother, uncles and aunties- when they die want you to continue with the duties that they used to perform for their devil worshiping. Inheriting nonsensical meaningless idolatry names, which start affecting our life, e.g. Mulindwa begets to Rwakaikara begets Alifaijo, Alifaijo begets Mbwa begets Mpisi begets Kahigwa begets Bitanaki, Byakunaga, Kazibona and Kadoma. They inherited you with shrines, witchcraft, idolatry Regalias like cowries, crowns with seashells, offertory baskets, vessels, obubugo costumes and spears.

Partaking food offered to idols yokes, eating food offered to idols. There are two different ways to eat food sacrificed to idols. One way is to actually partake of the sacrifice ritual in which the eater is giving honor and worship the idol. The Second way is to eat food of which a portion was first sacrificed to an idol without your knowledge. All the meat you buy in the market the animals are slaughtered by Moslems who face the animal to Mecca. In this way if you eat this meat you bought from the market you are not participating in the ritual sacrificed in directly. This is why you have to pray for any meal put before you. In some homes the first portion of every meal is laid before a statue of their idol or taken to the shrine first as a form of sacrifice or some satanists before they eat or drink any things they give offering to the ground.

Cursed and occultic places, by visiting places like going to attending Moslem festivals, funeral rituals, to watch procession of witches, idolatry March or procession, (embalu dance). If you go to sites of king's burial places, caves, shrine, ancestral grave sites or Occultic places like Cleopatra pyramids in Egypt. E.g. one day a lady who belonged to our church in 1980s they went to Hoima to for a crusade, after they visited a witch doctor's home who had a shrine she went into a shrine got hold of one of the ritual sticks and broke it. As she was breaking it she heard it breaking into her back bone and that was her beginning of trouble.

Gifts yokes, gifts from Occultic or satanic people that people may give you gift of some sort or money when you accept it, a curse of poverty or destruction is activated in your life. Occultic people may pretend to sell you something of an object specifically for used in satan's service as an attachment to get your money. Anoint the object and cleanse it the curse will be broken off it in the name of Jesus.

Refuse gifts from people you do not know well who mean good to you. At the Ranch in August 2010 a lady who was acting like a friend brought a friend to see me and another lady named Pauline from Nigeria. This lady was dressed in white and called herself a Doctor, she brought us gifts and for me more gifts, a perfume, a beautiful container in it there was a red beaded heart, but in the middle was a hidden pentagram. Immediately the Holy Spirit told me to throw the red heart away and give away the perfume and that is what I did. When I asked her whether she was a medical doctor she said she was a psychologist and that one day she wanted to be a psychiatrist.

Curses from God, parents, kings, witches and others, you can get a curse right from God, parent, Kings, witches and other people.

Curse from God, one can cause himself a curse of God, through rebellion you know you killed people, did witchcraft and instead of repenting you go and join a church which has no power to point out your sin; or you join a false doctrine or cult to cover up your past. You tell people that you are saved. I.e. one man was so involved in politics and in killings and the whole family was having bad reputation in killings and violence, as this family was involved to escape revenge, he joined a theological college and becomes a Clergyman to keep away his enemies. This does not work, one needs to repent and clean up all the dirt, still this kept him under bondage and keeps the whole family under God's curse.

Parent's curses, if one gets involved in Fight, quarrel or any other involvement which may cause a parent to curse you. "Your children and children of your children will also beat you as you have beaten me," one will suffer in life, he/she will never make any advancement.

King's curses, also if a king curses you, it is a strong curse. My grandfather who was an uncle to the king was keeping his royal cattle. One day when he was happy, he got the king's prize bull the king loved so much and slaughtered it and feasted on it with his servants. When the king came and asked for his prize bull it was no where. He cursed the old man so that he will not have cattle; he was having herds and herds of cattle but they all died and he died drinking water.

Witch's curse, one may go to witches and make agreements to take a sacrifice and then fails to take it as agreed, a witch doctor can utter a curse.

Curses from others like friends, relatives, even strangers, if one may fail to fulfill a promise or fail to give help at a time needed, i.e. one may be dying and wants to eat or drink something and you refuse to give it to them when you have it. A dying man may leave you a curse, i.e. one woman who was a cook for my dad could not eat millet, because a dying relative wanted to eat millet when she was very sick this woman refused to give it to her. Whenever she would start preparing millet meal she would start (Tyera!!! Tyera!!! and Biisi!!!).

Marriage bondages, one is born in a family with a chain of witchcraft and cannibals, they gets married to a family of night dancers or thieves. The children they get are double bondaged, one may study up to the highest education level still the devil will strike at any time he wants to strike, you have heard couples involved in accident on the way to reception, or ones hangs himself on the eve of his wedding day. (Justine case).

I had influential relatives who were held in high esteem in Tooro Kingdom, one even had Jet planes operating Nairobi to Zurich, Switzerland. His father was a County Chief, one of the Crown Bearers in the Palace who got married in 2 influential High clans which were idol worshipers. One of the wives was my aunt. He fathered more than 15 children who studied and became big officers in the army, teachers, managers, air hostesses and jet owners. When the name of that family was mentioned people would ask where you got to know that family? No one could guess that one day this family will never be by word or no more.

THE DEVIL IS VERY PATIENT, HE KNOWS HOW TO WAIT

The devil is very patient, he knows how to wait on traps of the ancestral covenants and agreements. When time comes, he starts to close in the web. That is why you need knowledge and facts when you are Born Again in order to jump these snares and traps, he set long ago through your ancestors.

Harvesting, this is when a family goes on and enjoy all the good time, children graduate marry and get married, get good jobs, then the evil one arrives. He waits for the fields to get ripe and start harvesting: In this family of my relatives this happened. The old man went and all the wives remaining to see the harvesting but the children started dropping one by one, accidents, AIDS, and tumors.

The man with jets who lived in Switzerland just dropped dead in London when he was not sick. The air-hostess collapsed and died in a plane just like that, then the old ladies also followed the next year dying one after another. Death without a good cause when a couple drove over the bridge and all died they were doctors and were coming from introduction. The bridge was broken and the villagers tried to stop them, but they paid no attention for reasons mot known but they just passed and plunged into the river.

A family of five on Masaka Road died in a car accident going or coming from burial. The enemy what he does to people who covenants with them when he gives them his money, he makes sure that they do not do something

Tangible, where one boasts and says at least I did something where people can remember me by. These people even though they had all the money, they did not do anything even to build family house that in case if there is a gathering. Though these people had all the riches which used to flow like a river, nothing was done at home. Mansions were built in London, Zurich, and Paris but not in Uganda.

The enemy makes your riches to be enjoyed by strangers instead of your own people. The enemy waits for you, if he does not hit there and then, he will wait for you to get married but victimize your family and children, by getting miscarriages, or you get children who die after a certain age by leukemia, sickle-cells or every time you give still births, or get children with fits, big heads, asthma, May wife gives birth to lion, hyena, stones, snakes, Albino, cancer, deformed, etc. I.e. my relative she was forced and got married even though I heard from the Lord Who told me to tell her not to marry the man she was going with. She thought I was jealousy. She got all the money her but she never got a child up to now.

These people under those bondages of an ancestor trap when they want to break off by coming to Jesus, the enemy cannot allow them to go to the right church with power to deliver, he will leads them to a powerless church which has no discernment, cult, wrong doctrine so that they cannot go to where these demons can be identified. So, they go to a wrong church which imitates the Bible Church, where they sit and think that all things are fine yet not.

Strangers will enjoy your riches, at times people decide to run away thinking that the enemy will not follow them, they run to Kampala, Kenya, London, or America where one may seem to prosper. Your prosperity will be enjoyed by strangers, but still if you have not got knowledge you will perish, the devil and his agents travel by wind he will find you there escaping from all that, get to the right Bible Teaching Church.

Poverty, families due to ancestral bondages and covenants they made may suffer the following: famine in the family, one will work so hard but achieve nothing even the food he grows in the garden will not yield so always will be spending money to buy food. And when he tries and break the line of poverty, bondage will come a form of fire and burn what ever stock you have in a shop or house market. If you break the yoke and survive, it may come in a form of lightning when your animals can be struck by Lightning. If you survive the rest may come in a form of thieves, your shop or house thieves will come once and carry everything and you go back to zero. Or, you will think every one is bewitching you and whatever you have so you go to witchdoctors to exchange witchcraft, they will demand chicken, goats, cows or whatever you have until you are left with nothing. (Encounter Orugwiso).

Source or roots of bondage and curses, there are several sources of bondage or curses that exist:

Inheritance, the sins of the forefathers they committed while still living thus witchcraft, idolatry, cannibalism, satan worshiping. Covenants, agreement, contracts they made with satan.

Broken dedication to satan, if you break dedication of what you used to give satan, if you stop giving respect you used to give to the devil, that is breaking your dedication.

Ancestors acceptance of bondage or curses on

the lives of descendants, this is in the case of the Jews when they killed Jesus they said "let His blood be on us and our grand children." Parents, grandparents may swear that their children and grandchildren will continue with the devil or satanic rituals even if they are no longer living.

Involvement with unclean and unholy things, this is when one plays with unholy things. You can get witchcraft objects left for a purpose and you start playing with them.

13th - 17th July 2009

CHAPTER 25
SET YOURSELF FREE

PROCESS TO SET Yourself Free From Satanic Covenants

Past History, get all the information concerning your ancestors, grandparents, parents and all your past involvement of any kind you know which could have opened a door for bondage. Ignorance is no excuse.

Repentance, you need to repent from whatever sins you have committed consciously and unconsciously, every sin you do is done against God.

Be specific, identify the particular covenants you are breaking. There are different types of covenants, bondages, agreements to break like intermarriage covenants, covenants of death (cannibalism) exchange, blood covenants, (Omukago).

Be scriptural, use the Word of God as the basis of your spiritual warfare. Just as everything positive was created by the Word, so everything negative can be destroyed by the invocation of the Word of God.

Be systematic, concentrate on breaking the covenants before moving on to curses, because curses are results of covenants. Covenants are Agreements made and curses are the products of these agreements. Covenants must be Broken before the curses are broken.

Be aggressive, pray with determination, steadfast, bold and resolute. Believe in the power of the Word of God in your mouth to nullify whatever agreements that satan holds against you.

Be spontaneous, deal with whatever the Holy Spirit drops in your heart when you may not have been aware of, the Holy Spirit can lead you to deal covenants you did not know of, e.g. in my early time of salvation in dreams the Holy Spirit used to bring me snakes, then centipedes as big and as long and big as a train, and those were my ancestral snake demons they used to worship. I continued breaking those ancestral covenants year after year until they could no longer come to visit me.

THERE IS NOT ANY AMOUNT OF FASTING AND PRAYER, confession and speaking in tongues that can release the person from an evil covenant if the person does not stand their ground, and unless you stand your ground, to disentangle themselves. They will always confess they are saved but not living a life of breakthrough in so many areas. When you are still under this bondage these things will happen to you.

CHAPTER 26

BLASPHEMOUS AND ABUSIVE SONGS

BLASPHEMOUS AND ABUSIVE Songs in the Christian Churches

How people of God are comparing and contrasting God with the things He created. Thou shall not make image, paint, compare me with anything in heaven under world or on the earth, Exodus 20:4.

"I am God." He told Moses "I am Who I am" Exodus. 3:14. People are singing "You are on top of the witches, harlots, wealthy men," or "You are better than Gold, Silver." I feel Him in my waist, head, knees. Jesus, God created all those with a Word "Let there be, and everything came into being." The enemy has entered into the Church and is abusing and blaspheming God. The devil is throwing bait through music and people grab it without knowing what they are doing, and dance on the blasphemous abusive music the evil one has brought in the church. Let us be careful of everything which is done in the church because the enemy has his agents there. You will not know until it is too late that you were breaking the 1st Commandment. God does not change on His Word. *19th July 2009*

Appointing, the Lord spoke to me in terms of appointing. He said many people are appointing themselves. He calls them but before He prepares them they jump and start calling themselves names, e.g. Apostle, Pastor, Prophets, etc. before He names them. At times they are even changing their calling to another calling.

He asked me a question: Doesn't President Musebeni appoint ambassadors, ministers, and permanent secretaries? Can one just come up in the morning and say "I am Ambassador of London," or can one wake up in the morning and say "I am a Minister of Education," without being appointed to that post?

If people of the world follow the orders why do not people of the Kingdom of God do the their same. For the President to appoint people in his government first he has to consider 1. Educational qualifications, 2. Commitment to the Party, 3. Relationship with the people of the constituency, etc.

The same principles apply to the Kingdom of God, before one is appointed certain things have to be considered, e.g. Knowledge of the Word, Prayer Life, Commitment to the Lord, Ministry and Fellowship with Brethren. 21st July, 2009

> *Prayer, I pray Lord, may You grant me more time to commune with you on the Altar of my soul than the time I spend with my own interests. Lord, I need to seek You more than anything else. Lord, let my latter days be more fruitful, I will seek you more, love you more, pray to you more, and serve you more. Lord, whenever the*

enemy tries to lie to me by taking me back to old places where covenants, agreements, contracts were made, may the Holy Spirit empower me and utilize the opportunity so that I will destroy those scenes at the enemy's cost. Amen. 1st August 2009

OUR LORD TOLD BRO RICK JOYNER AS WRITTEN IN The Call, What Brings Joy to Our Father's Heart? When the least of the brethren on the earth shows Him love. When a humble church sings to our Father with true love in their hearts our Father silences all of heaven to listen to them. When those who are living in such darkness and difficulty sing with true hearts to Him. It touches Him more than all of the myriads of heaven can. A few holy ones struggling to express their adoration for Him.

Our Lord told Rick that every time I see My brethren touch my Father with true worship, it makes the pain and grief I knew on the cross seem like a small price to pay. He said "Nothing brings Me more joy than when you worship my Father." I went to the cross so that you could worship Him through Me. It is in this worship that you, the Father and I are all One. Our Father's glory is seen when all the angels cannot help it but to worship. When you worship without seeing His glory in the midst of your trials that is worship in spirit and in truth. Do not waste your trials. Worship the Father, not for what you will receive, but to bring Him joy.

You will never be stronger than when you bring Him Joy, for the Joy of the Lord is your strength. 7th *August 2009*

God is so great to Him the sun is like an atom, a very small thing, and the galaxies like the grains of sand, yet He listens to our prayers and often grieving for us. Every human being has power to cause Him joy or pain.

There should be no moment wasted if you know that it could be spent worshipping Him. Our Father gets greater joy when one worships Him when He is in greater trials or darkness it touches Him more. It made Bro Rick go receive trials so that he could worship Him through them. Job said when he met God "I used only to know You by just hearing in the ears, and now I have seen You, I repent in dust and ashes."

Jesus told Rick "Remember the potential for even the least of my little ones to touch the heart of the Father. That alone makes their value greater than any price. Let the children come to me, Jesus said He would have gone to the cross again for a single one of these. He said "I feel the pain and the joy of every soul, I know your trials because we share them."

"The greatest worship and greatest expression of faith that pleases Him will come to us in the midst of trials."

The Lord says "I will come to you in different people, different circumstances. Your highest purpose is to recognize Me, to hear My voice and Follow Me." He knows how, when and through whom to speak to you, like the book of Isaiah when I was in a dilemma. Those through whom He speaks to you are part of the message called testimonies. The greatest calling of all is to be fully conquered by Him, e.g. Apostle Paul.

"You cannot measure eternal treasures on the earth." You will not measure true spiritual fruit rightly while you are on the earth, only you can measure your true success by how much more clearly you are able to behold the Lord, by how much better you know His Voice and by how much more you love the brethren." Your victory in life will be according to your desire for Him.

Never measure yourself by others comparing yourself with

others, but keep pressing forward. Seeking more of Him. "Do not boast in your strength but in your weaknesses. If you will openly talk more about your failure in order to help others, I will be able to openly display your victories, for whoever will exalt himself shall be humbled, and he who humbles himself shall be exalted. Humility, you can humble yourself; by falling on the rock and being broken, or the rock falling on you and crushing you to powder; either way, the final results will be brokenness which is humility. Humility is the opposite of Pride; pride always results in tragedy, darkness and suffering. When you start being embarrassed it is because you are beginning to move to pride. A humble person cannot be embarrassed; learn to embrace every opportunity to be humble and listen to His instructions, (Heathrow Experience of Kora Sidika).

Ask the Lord for a mantle of Humility, and never take it off, whenever you take it off you become spiritually blind and deaf. Pride blinds and deafens so you cannot see or hear clearly and when you are proud because it puffs up your head. The mantle will shield you from focusing on yourself and when satan took his first step into self-seeking and pride a multitude of God's angels God had entrusted to his authority followed him; same as after Adam's fall the world's multitude suffered. When you are humble God entrusts you with His Authority which goes with responsibility. There can be no true authority without responsibility. This means that others will suffer if you go wrong. "The more authority you are given, the more that you can either help or hurt others by your actions." You are part of the new creation that is much higher than the first creation. Those who are called to rule with Jesus are given the greatest responsibility of all. They are called to a position higher than satan held. He was a great angel, but he was not a son. You are called to be a joint heir with Jesus.

Our whole life, both the trials and the revelations, are for the purpose of teaching us the responsibility of authority. Our whole life, both the trials and the revelations, are all for the purpose of teaching us the responsibility of authority.

Adonijah boasted that his father, king David, did not discipline him. Solomon complained that he could not get away with anything without his father's discipline. David disciplined Solomon, he knew that Solomon was called to be a king. Even in the Kingdom of God, those who are disciplined are those who are on a walk of greater authority. *9th August 2009*

CHAPTER 27

END TIME, SPIRITUAL WARFARE,

END TIME, Spiritual WarFare, We are living in the time of Warfare in Battle! Who is Fighting who? Always a battle or warfare engages two parties. Which are the two forces Fighting? The huge dragon was thrown out, that ancient serpent called the devil or satan that deceived the whole world was thrown down to earth and all his angels with him, Revelations 12:9-10.

The Lord's People and Satanic Forces, with the tail he dragged a third of the stars out of the sky and threw them down to the earth. Rev. 12:4, 9. Why are they Fighting? The dragon, satan, devil was furious with the woman and went off to Fight against the rest of her descendants, all those who obey God's Commandments and are faithful to the truth revealed by Jesus. Revelations 12:17.

Therefore, Christian are Fighting: To Keep the Commandments of God, To hold the testimony of Jesus, To do the Will of God, To Win Souls for the Lord and To focus on Christ. Jesus said I am the Way, the Truth and the Life. No one goes to the Father except by me, John 14:6.

The Satanic Forces are at war: To stop the Christians from

Keeping the Commandments of God, Rev. 12:17, To stop the Testimony of Jesus, To stop Christians who do the Will of God, To stop Christians from Winning Souls for Christ, and To stop them from focusing on Christ, John 14:6.

Before we get to war, we have to identify the strengths and weaknesses of the weapons the enemy has, his position and strategies. Remember we can never outsmart the devil, the Word says "Resist the devil and he will flee." We should train our committed members by having seminars, workshops, and teaching sessions. These are for Pastors, Intercessors, Deacons, Elders, Youth Leaders and youth, and in this Warfare, our Commander is Jesus, He is giving us instructions: when to Camp, when to March and when to Fight. We have to obey His instructions or else the enemy will destroy us. In this warfare, if we disobey instructions, we will be destroyed like Achan, the Old Prophet of Bethel in Joshua 7:5,24, and the Prophet from Judah in 1 Kings 13:9,17-24.

In this warfare the world's battle focus is on the Born Agains. Whenever something happens to Born Again people they are directly Fighting for God. The warfare is physical now and demons are appearing in physical ways.

Bases of Warfare, Corrupt Mind, in order to Fight effectively in this Warfare, we need first to deal with our Corrupt Minds. The mind is so corrupt and it is contributing much to the Warfare, because Christians are still living carnally they cannot Fight and win the battle because the enemy is their comrade in crime, In order to enter in warfare we have to clear our corrupted mind. The mind is so corrupt even if you spend 50 years in salvation, it might never be a changed. A convict in prison if he or she gets so saved without dealing with the corrupt mind, after being released will be back in prison the following week.

Some identified areas of corrupt mind, blessed is the man who walks not in the counsel of the wicked, nor stands in the way of sinners, nor sits in the seat of scoffers, Psalms 1:1 (ESV); Do not be conformed to this world, but be transformed by the renewal of your mind, that by testing you may discern what is the will of God, what is good and acceptable and perfect, Romans 12:2 (ESV).

Mind-set, Hallo Effects, it is wrong thinking, set on a particular situation, e.g. one sees a boy walking with a girl, automatically starts thinking, they are coming from A, B, C, D, they may be colleagues or a sister and brother. Wrong thoughts originate from evil: they are perceived thoughts driven by evil to do wrong, once the evil has entered one cannot settle down and feels uneasy, John 1 3 2, 27.

Wrong thoughts from evil create a hurry! Hurry!! attitude of impatience and makes a person forget the promises, Rebecca forgot what the Lord told her that "The older will serve the younger," Gen. 25:23. Rebecca carried on her corrupt plans, yet the Lord would have brought it to pass at the right time for the promise to come without running away from home to the extent not seeing his son grow into a man and not burying his mother and his father for the fear of Esau, Gen. 27:5-19. .

Expectations and anticipations, these are ideas people expect and anticipate evil, against a person. One says, "I knew this was going to happen long before." At times evil thoughts can go ahead and kill when a murderous spirit is in possession of a person's corrupt, e.g. one lady was walking on a rainy day and a car passed and splashed muddy water on her; she said "I wish I find you crashed down the hill" and it was as she said, down the hill the man crashed.

Desires, are in born corrupt minds, desiring to see somebody in trouble. A woman in a church with her grandchild of 14 years had got pregnant by a boy from a poor family and she knew she was not going to benefit by asking for over and above assistance. She said "instead my granddaughter being pregnant by Tom, she should be pregnant by Moses." One day in the village a young man died and his grandmother did not know that my mom was in the next room. She said "every time they are bringing coffins of my children, when will one for Kabatalemwa also come?" My mom replied "Kabatalemwa befriended God so you will not see her coffin."

Imaginations, these are imaginary thoughts which originate in a corrupt mind, like when one imagines someone being killed in accident or imagines his enemy being buried. Because of much hatred one can even go and take announcement to the Radio announcing the death of a living person.

Wrong motives are intentions geared towards creating evil scenes in one's mind, e.g. one may intentionally try to woo a girl for an AIDS case man, so that he infects her with AIDS and she dies. One cannot live with a corrupt mind like this and Fight and win in Warfare because you are a partner with the devil. Rom. 12:2; Jealousy, anger, hatred, and shame, Gen. 4:4-5, if anger corrupts you, a spirit of anger sits on you and starts breeding poisonous thoughts of murder, suicide or witchcraft.

This hated, anger or jealousy causes your thoughts to brew poison in your system, which later can result committing the above offenses. In most cases if one does not blow out and takes it inward, it will cause one to go insane, madness, ulcers, heart diseases, cancer, blood sugar and at times fits. Anger or jealousy affects your breathing system where your muscles lock up and you get blood flow disorder. Our system is like a running water, the more you give it a passage it will continue running freely but when you block it, either it will look for where to break through or it will be stagnant and get polluted with whatever falls there will stay, decay and rotten later start to smell. Release anger immediately by repenting, forgiving, ignoring or making peace with the one who has angered you.

HOW TO FIGHT THE CORRUPT MIND

The six types of corrupt mind can be driven out with: the Word of God, command the demons of mind corruption to leave! 2 Cor. 10:3

Sing songs of Praise and Worship when attacked by corrupt thoughts. Seek the Lord in Fasting and Prayer. Go for Total Deliverance to a Church with that Ministry. Pray without ceasing and give corrupt thoughts no time. Make a covenant with God for: 1. all your Family, and Church, Zech. 9:11; 2. Business; 3. Property; and 4. possessions, Job, Genesis 12:1-3, Genesis 17:1-7, Exodus 6:5, Joshua 1:8.

I perceived that whatever God does endures forever; nothing can be added to it, nor anything taken from it. God has done it, so that people fear before him. Ecclesiastes 3:14.

All in all, cover them with the Blood of Jesus Christ.

16th August 2009

CHAPTER 28

I CAN STEAL THAT SHEEP FROM YOU

AN OLD MAN took his son to go and be trained as a professional thief. After the boy completed his training One day he met the old man with sheep, he told the old

Man "I am a trained thief, I can steal that sheep from you." The old man said, you cannot steal it from me even if you are trained. The boy went a head of the man and the sheep, he was wearing new shoes, after when he turned the corner, he removed one shoe and dropped it in the middle of the path and ran a head in the bush.

When the old man with the sheep came and saw it he was so disappointed because it was so beautiful and it was only one. He continued on his journey, the boy ran a head and hid in the bush and dropped another shoe in the middle of the road. When the old man arrived, he was so happy to find the second shoe matching with the first one. The old man decided to tie the sheep on the side of the road and go to fetch the other shoe. The boy untied the sheep and ran with it.

WHEN THE OLD MAN RETURNED THE SHEEP WAS NOWHERE.

Never turn for the lost chance. If you wanted to marry a lady or a man one time and things did not go well, leave her and continue looking ahead. Leave the bygone and look straight ahead, God has carried the best ahead of you and the failures have remained behind.

Then the boy came and found the boys he trained with to be thieves and told them the story and they were amused. He said he was taking the sheep to his father who paid for his training.

The other thieves said you cannot take it to him we are the ones who trained you, the boy was over powered and they said we are killing the sheep and to have a barbecue now.

The boy said I think I am more professional than you and I can steal this sheep from you! They said impossible, already they had removed its head, they removed the offals and commanded him to go and wash them at the brook. As the boy was washing the offals he hatched a plan to steal the meat from them.

He went ahead and broke a stick and started beating the water and at the same time crying swiftly he cried, No do not kill me! I am not the one who stole the sheep! Those who stole the sheep are up there with the meat! When the other thieves heard that, they took off and left the meat, the boy went up and collected the meat and took it to his father.

The devil is tricky, never underestimate him, he has so many lies, but you can overcome him but only by trusting in the Lord at all times. 20th *August 2009*

CHAPTER 29

MY FRIEND - WHO IS THE WICKED PERSON?

COME CLOSE TO THE LORD WHILE HE IS NEAR

KASESE CRUSADE - SEEK the Lord while He may be found: Call Him while He is near, Isaiah 55:6-7.

The Lord is closer to you than you are close to your Heart because He resides in you, He has set eternity into our hearts. Eccl. 3:11.

Samson would tear a lion in pieces because of eternity in him. The foxes gathered in one place for Him to get them tails by tail and set fire and send them in the fields of the Philistines. He killed 1000 Philistines with the jaw of a donkey. The madman of Gerasene had a Legion residing in him, where are all those demons lodged, in the eternity.

Eternity depends on how you use it, if you choose the evil way, or when you Choose to be good! Call upon Him while He is near!!! So the Lord is in your heart, "The Word is Near You in your mouth and in your Heart" so that if you confess with your mouth Jesus is Lord and believe in your heart that God raised Him from the dead, you will be saved. For with the heart a person believes, resulting in righteousness and with the mouth he confesses, resulting in salvation, Romans 10:8-10.

It is today you can come close to God and He will save you before you are called either for heaven or Eternal Doom.

> *Mukama akuhaire obwire,*
> *Ozire ebibi byawe Ojunwe,*
> *Baitu iwe Omalirire*
> *Okoole bihweyo ,*
> *nukwo Ohwerekerre.*
>
> *Ensi'eyesamire, kumira*
> *Abaamwangire!!*
> *Akaire ko kyaroho!!!*
> *Ija omwikirize ojunweeeeeeeee!!*
>
> *You have been given time*
> *Repent and be born again but*
> *You've decided to sin to the end,*
> *And face eternal Doom*
>
> *I see!! the open pit,*
> *To swallow His enemies*
> *Come now the time is here*
> *And be born again!*

Let the wicked forsake his way and the unrighteous man his thoughts; and let him return to the Lord!!! My friend who is the wicked person? The wicked person is the one who thinks evil, talks evil, and does evil. His whole being is brewed with evil.

Expectations and anticipations, these are ideas where people expect and anticipate evil against another person. One says, "I knew this was going to happen long before." At times evil thoughts can go ahead and kill when a murderous spirit is in possession of a corrupt minded person, e.g. one lady was walking on a rainy day and a car passed and splashed muddy water on her, she said "I wish I find you crashed down the hill" and it was as she said, down the hill the man crashed.

Desires, when one is born with corrupt mind and desires to see somebody in trouble. A woman in church with her grand child of 14 years who got impregnated by a boy from a poor family where she new she was not going to benefit by asking for over and above assistance. She said "instead my granddaughter to be impregnated by Tom, she should have been pregnant by Moses." One day in the village a young man died, his grandmother did not know that my mom was in the next room. She said "every time they are bringing coffins of children, when will the one of Kabatalemwa also come?"

My mom replied, "Kabatalemwa befriended God, you will not see her coffin."

Imaginations, these are imaginary thoughts which originates in a corrupt mind, one imagines one being killed in accident or imagines his enemy being buried. Because of much hatred one can even go and take announcement to the Radio announcing the death of a living person.

Wrong motives, are intensions geared towards creating evil tendencies: one may intentionally try to woo a girl for an AIDS case man, so that he affects her with AIDS and she dies. One cannot live with a corrupt mind like this and Fight and win in Warfare because this one is a partner with the devil, Romans 12:2.

Jealousy, anger, hatred, and shame, Gen. 4:4-5, when anger corrupts you a spirit of anger sits on you and starts breeding poisonous thoughts of murder, suicide or witchcraft. This anger or jealousy causes your thoughts to brew poison in your system which later can result committing the above offenses. In most cases, if one does not blow out and takes it inward it will cause one insane madness, ulcers, heart disease, cancer, blood sugar or at times fits. Anger and jealousy effects your breathing system your muscles locks up and you get blood flow disorder. Our system is like a running water, the more you give it a passage it will continue running freely, but the moment you block it, either it will look for where to break through or it will be stagnant and get polluted with whatever falls there will stay and rot there and start smelling.

A wicked person is like the raven that Noah sent, it never came back because if found the dead bodies and started eating so that it never returned to the Ark. But when the dove was sent it came back when it could not light on anything, because the dove is a clean bird it does not eat rotten things. So, when evil people find people back biting, discussing arsenal, ManU, TV, exciting sex, violent movies, Nigerian movies, etc. they sit and enjoy and forget to return to the Ark.

But when good people go out and find people gossiping, they cannot sit and listen because that is not their kind of food for their Souls; they run back towards the Ark and Noah puts up the hand and returns them to the Ark.

The righteous person is the one who thinks good, talks good, does good. His whole being is brewed with good. His and her life is full of goodness. Prayer is food for their soul, they seeks after God in righteousness. They avoid prayers of seeking after the worldly things like vehicles, houses, and money because they know that God is their father and all that belongs to Him. Seek ye first the Kingdom of God.

They seek inner beauty instead of outer beauty, e.g. hairdos, painting themselves, they avoid all that wastes their time for the Lord. Revelation of John Mulinde about the bell ringing in

Heaven that some lady's hair was entangled in the barbed wire, they could not run faster with high heeled shoes, their dressing was improper, etc.

Brethren let us seek for eternal things and not these worldly riches which are for only today and tomorrow then you face eternal doom.

Banywani nyowe binsobire
Bantu tiba kyatina Mukama
Nibaserra ebyabu habwabu
Habwitungo lyensi.

Fellows I am so perturbed!!!
There is no fear of the Lord
People seeking after their own
For perishing riches!

Remedy, release anger immediately by repenting, forgiving, ignoring or making peace with the one who has angered you!

How to Fight the corrupt mind, For though we live in the world, we do not wage war as the world does, 2 Corinthians 10:3. The corrupt mind can be driven out with a Word of God, command the demons of corruption to leave mind. Sing songs of Praise and Worship when attacked by corrupt thoughts. Seek the Lord in Fasting and Prayer. Go for Total Deliverance to a Church with that Ministry. Pray without ceasing and give corrupt thoughts no time. Leave people who do not help you to see God more clearly Genesis 12:1-3. Quit family, clan, friends, or jobs which become a stumbling block to see God clearly

The way to heaven is a solitary walk, you walk it alone not a group, No! No! it's not an easy way! No! No, it's not easy, But Jesus walks beside me and Brightens the way and lightens every heavy load. Be obedient to God and make a covenant with God,

Genesis 17:1-7; Zech. 9:11; even a covenant with God for your children, your Family, Church, job, and business. Remember God will always remember the Covenant He made with you, Exodus 6:5;

Let the Word of God never depart from you day and Night, Joshua 1:8;

If you keep all what the Lord tells you He will establish you in all your under takings, Ecclesiastes 3:14.

Cover them all with the Blood of Jesus Christ. *1st September 2009*

CHAPTER 30
THE TRULY SPIRITUAL MAN

THE TRULY SPIRITUAL MAN IS ODD/STRANGE, NOT UNDERSTOOD, MISTAKEN ALWAYS:

- Lives not for self - so stop building your own empire
- Promotes the interest of others – Look where to assist other ministries
- Pleads to people to give all to the Lord – Tell people to walk right for the Lord
- Asks no portion or share for self – Don't ask help from people tell God
- Delights not to be honoured but – Don't make show of yourself
- To see the Saviour glorified in the eyes of others – but lift the name of Jesus
- The Lord promoted and self-neglected – Talk much about the Lord and not Self
- Is often silent in the midst of NOISE religious shop talk – Don't urge with people about God

- Referred as dull and over serious, a gulf between her and society widens – People will call you names; self-righteous, saint, impotent... etc
- Searchers for friends of the same mind and finds few or none, like Mary of old keeps these things in her heart – May not find people who understanding you in the things of God...
- Seeks to understand the Saviour more intimately – Seek God in the most intimate way: reading more of His Word, denials, fasting, praying and having intimate time with Him
- Heartbroken for the Lord and after righteousness – Cultivate more time to seek after righteousness.
- Has many trials but not shaken by them, eyes fixed on the Lord – The bigger the trials the great the Testimony
- Is a topic of everybody, as they seek to break into their secret cover – people will group and talk much about you because they want to discover your secret hiding
- Is not easily penetrated – You will safeguard the Lord's Secrets. Some are to be given others are not to be shared
- Has on, a robe of humility which attracts no one but only the Giver – you do not try to attract anybody but only the Maker. To get this robe, one author said "You have to fall on the rock and be broken or the rock to fall on you and crush you."
- Self-denial for the sake of seeking righteousness – The Lord may tell you to do something which may help you to gain in spiritual life (Hair DO & eye shadows) I was watching series of Nephilim Spirits in Musicians they talked about heavy duty make up and deep eye shadows are demonic it comes from the pit

- Does not discuss affairs of others for slander – Avoid discussing affairs of the brethren (Gossip)
- Cares for the interest of others
- Is fulfilled when others are happy – You do not feel jealousy (Enugu) when others get promoted, succeeds (but some people can even get hurt when they see you have no tendencies of jealousy)

MESSAGE: JEREMIAH 15:19, ISAIAH 54:9 - 11, AND PSALM 50:16-22. 2nd - 6th September 2009

God Disturbs the Present to Improve the Future

DR TRULIN, MORRIS CERULLO
MINISTRIES

MY TRIALS, PETER'S DISAPPEARANCE AND APPEARANCE, then Robert disappeared to strengthen My faith in the Lord.

Landing runway and clearance on the visit of John Glass from Europe to Victory Church, he preached on the "Extension of the Landing Runway and Terminal." In September 2009 LA Airport was planning to spend $50 million to expand the runways and terminals to handle bigger aircrafts. Therefore, on this note he asked people to expand and clear their runways to handle what the Holy Spirit is in process to bring to those who are ready to receive the Lord's blessings.

As he was preaching, it came to my mind that; on the runway

there should not be stones, sticks, or animals crossing; therefore, the runway has to be completely clear. This represents our life, we have to keep it clear by repenting, or picking up the stones, sticks and chasing animals and birds which may hold the Holy Spirit from landing. Our Runway should be well marked and lit, when the Holy Spirit aircrafts want to land there It will not be meet obstacles. Your runway is full of stones and sticks, thus unforgiveness, gossip, stealing, fornication, battles within you, they hinder the Holy Spirit to land on your Runway. 3rd *October 2009*

FOR YOUR BEAUTIFUL GARDEN PUT A CLEARANCE

For your beautiful garden put a clearance (Nsaro), between your beautiful garden and the next bush, the beautiful garden is your soul. You need to keep a distance, so that the scorch and creeping grass will not creep into your garden, because they move quietly and steadily. But if you have kept a distance as they try to cross, you will cut them before they enter your garden, i.e. my dad used to enjoy gardening but in his garden he would have a clearance of 3 feet wide and would plant tough grass to deter the scorch creeping grass to stop the cross to his well kept garden, also to stop soil erosion.

    Therefore, you be principled in character, which may guard you, even if one try to jump over or try to penetrate you will they will find tough grass (Pasplam). When she or he brings gossip about others say, "You know I do not entertain such talks, can we talk about something else?" Look at somebody and give her a look that spells "I am not ready to listen to that," the scorch, leeches and creepy grass will be chopped midway.

When your beautiful garden is neighboring a bush, there are snakes, rats, creeping and flying insects which may keep visiting your garden. Be on the alert for these visits to your garden. I had an experience in our Office at Amber House one time we had an opposite neighbor who proved to be a Lawyer by profession, but the people who used to occupy that office were not all good. In our office we serve fruits, juice, soda and water and many times they would cross over to get themselves a drink or a fruit. When you have your beautiful garden keep an open eye fixed on the bush next to your garden.

One day, came a white man who claimed to be a Bishop. Earlier on I had met him on the street before he came to the lawyer's office, and the Holy Spirit spoke to me that "He has problems." I looked back as he walked towards Speke Hotel. After two weeks as I was in my office. I saw him standing outside my office and I recognized him and went to ask him if he needed help. When he came to my office, he poured his problems to me, I kind of helped him by giving him a drink and gave him 5,000 for transport because he told me he used to walk all the way from Entebbe, on empty stomach, that he used to go for days without food. After some time, he started to come to the lawyer's office, this man claimed to be a bishop, but to my surprise, he was behaving in unbecoming manner with street girls he used to receive in the Lawyer's office and would hang around and later started to come around our office to get themselves a drink or fruits. From that time I completely disassociated with him.

KEEP YOUR GARDEN PROTECTED.

I had made a clearance around my garden, so no snakes, rats, or monkeys could enter my Garden.

Keep your garden protected. Some come as sisters and

brothers who even may tell you that they have been in the faith for such a long time but have never grown up. Put on a guard and say; so far and no further, many people are now looking how to penetrate into your life, they want to know how deep you are in salvation, or how they can use you and exploit you and say, "Hey. you are saved?" You are not supposed to say "not;" whenever they ask because you are saved, so that they cheat you and you keep quiet.

Sir, Madam, give them a distance, calculate what you say; Your enemy the devil prowls roaring like a roaring lion looking for whom to devour, 1 Peter 5:8.

The Farm

*Nyamabuga Foundation Schools in 2018.
Our school has more than 400 students*

LEARN MORE AT WWW.NEEPUGANDA.ORG

ABOUT THE AUTHOR

The late Gertrude Kabatalemwa labored for the kingdom of God in her native land of Uganda. The burden of her heart was for the good news of Jesus to become deeply rooted, firmly grounded, and abundantly fruitful in the lives of the people of Uganda. In the past, she has served her nation as secretary to the president. She also functioned as Minister for the Development of Women.

At one point, she had taken in thirty-five of the orphans into her own village home, subsequently establishing Nyamabuga Foundational Schools for village children. Her plans include to prepare and equip these young people with the skills necessary to be able to lead their nation with a moral worldview.

Today, her children and those that she has poured into continue her work.

Through this book, you will be blessed by encountering the very large heart of this precious servant of God.

This is Ms. Kabatalemwa's first of the six book series "My Deepest Heart's Devotions."

facebook.com/Neepuganda

www.ingramcontent.com/pod-product-compliance
Lightning Source LLC
Chambersburg PA
CBHW052131110526
44591CB00012B/1677